BRIDGE BIDDING

LESSONS AND QUIZZES ON GOREN'S

POINT COUNT METHOD

John Mallon

Illustrated with Easy-to-Read Diagrams of Bridge Hand

NEW, REVISED EDITION

Introduction by Charles H. Goren

COLLIER BOOKS
A Division of Macmillan Publishing Co., Inc.
NEW YORK

COLLIER MACMILLAN PUBLISHERS
LONDON

This revised Collier Books edition is published by arrangement with Abelard-Schuman, Limited. Macmillan Publishing Co., Inc., 866 Third Avenue, New York, N.Y. 10022. Collier-Macmillan Canada Ltd. Printed in the United States of America.

Introduction

TEACHING by trial and error is by no means a new technique, but the manner in which it has been accomplished by Mr. Mallon in this book is especially worthy of note.

Just as in any language some 850 simple, basic words have been found sufficient for normal, every day exchange of ideas and information; in the same way the knowledge of a comparatively few fundamental principles and simple rules of bidding will usually enable a player to understand and make himself understood at the bridge table.

Over a period of years I have attempted to devise a bridge language complete enough to permit the full exchange of ideas and yet simple enough to be grasped readily by the veriest tyro. The success which has greeted this effort has been most gratifying and Mr. Mallon's splendid collection of quizzes has furthered the cause. It has been my observation that the most effective manner of teaching is the use of actual bridge hands. It seems easier to draw principles from cases than to make cases conform to principles. It is for this reason that the quiz has been as essential part of every book I have written.

The student will find this manual very interesting, and it can hardly fail to be helpful.

CHARLES H. GOREN

Contents

Foreword

THE GOREN POINT COUNT method of bidding is like a simple language in which each player tells his partner how strong his hand is, and in what suit his strength lies. If this information is given and understood correctly, the partners will arrive at the proper contract.

This book is offered as a text for learning or teaching the Goren Point Count method of bidding.

Every effort has been made to make this study as easy as possible. The principles and rules are condensed and simplified, but not to such an extent that accuracy is sacrificed—except in unimportant details.

The material is logically arranged in 29 short lessons. In each lesson, because of the format, the essential instructions stand out and will stick in the reader's memory. Where bridge hands are shown, they can be visualized without effort, because they look like bridge hands.

The first part of this book consists of the 29 lessons, which cover all the essential bidding situations that arise in the game of Contract Bridge. Each lesson explains a basic principle of the Goren method, and gives a condensed rule to follow in bidding.

The second part of this book consists of 36 bridge hands, illustrating quizzes which cover all bidding situations.

The last part of this book gives a short summary of the bidding rules.

PART ONE

LESSONS

IN THE FALL OF 1957 Goren announced certain changes in his system. In the light of these changes Lessons 10, 11, 25, and 26 have been revised in this edition of *Bridge Bidding*.

Lessons 10 and 11 cover responses and rebids after an opening bid of 1 No trump. Lessons 25 and 26 cover the jump overcall and responses to a jump overcall. If the instructions in these lessons are followed, your bids will be understood both by an advanced partner and by a partner who has not kept up-to-date.

In other lessons certain refinements in the system, announced in 1957, have been noted for the benefit of the advanced player.

No instructions have been included on two innovations, the "Unusual No trump" and the "Gerber 4-Club Convention," because the opportunity to use these purely artificial bids arises so seldom.

Lesson 1

THE POINT COUNT

There are 2 kinds of points in a bridge hand—points counted for high cards and points counted for distribution.

Points assigned for high cards

Count 4 points for each Ace. Count 3 points for each King. Count 2 points for each Queen. Count 1 point for each Jack.

Points assigned for distribution

When bidding a suit of your own: Count 1 point for each doubleton. Count 2 points for each singleton. Count 3 points for each void.

When raising a suit bid by your partner: Count 1 point for each doubleton. Count 3 points for each singleton. Count 5 points for each void.

When bidding No trump and responding to No trump bids: Do not count any points for doubletons, singletons, or voids.

When responding to opening bid of 1 No trump: In addition to the points you count for high cards, count 1 extra point, if the hand contains a five-card or longer suit.

Points required for game and slams

The number of points in your hand and your partner's hand combined will determine how many tricks you and your partner together can take.

With 26 points you can usually make a game in No trump.

With 26 points you can usually make a game in a major suit.

With 29 points you can usually make a game in a minor suit.

With 33 points you can usually make a small slam.

With 37 points you can usually make a grand slam.

Points

POINTS FOR HIGH CARDS
A - 4   K - 3   Q - 2   J - 1

POINTS FOR DISTRIBUTION

When Bidding Your Own Suit		When Raising Partner's Suit
1 point -	Doubleton -	1 point
2 points -	Singleton -	3 points
3 points -	Void - - -	5 points

When Responding to Bid of 1 No trump
Add 1 point for a 5-card or longer suit

POINTS REQUIRED

26 - game in No trump	33 - small slam
26 - game in major suit	37 - grand slam
29 - game in minor suit	

HOW MANY POINTS DO YOU HOLD?

1 You dealt the cards.
It is your opening bid.

ANSWERS

1 Your hand contains 12 points. Count 4 for the A of Hearts, 3 for the K of Clubs, 2 for the Q of Diamonds, 3 for the void in Spades.

HOW MANY POINTS DO YOU HOLD?

2 You dealt the cards.
It is your opening bid.

3 You dealt the cards.
It is your opening bid.

4 You dealt the cards.
It is your opening bid.

5 Your partner opened 1 No trump.
Your right hand opponent passed.

6 Your partner opened 1 Heart.
Your right hand opponent passed.

7 Your partner opened 1 Diamond.
Your right hand opponent passed.

ANSWERS

2 Your hand contains 12 points. Count 1 for the J of Hearts, 4 for the A of Clubs, 3 for the K of Diamonds, 2 for the Q of Diamonds, 2 for the singleton in Spades.

3 Your hand contains 16 points. Count 4 for the A of Spades, 3 for the K of Hearts, 1 for the J of Hearts, 4 for the A of Clubs, 2 for the Q of Diamonds, 1 for the J of Diamonds, 1 for the doubleton in Spades. If, however, you are considering opening with a bid of 1 No trump, you can count only 15 points, because you cannot count points for short suits in evaluating your hand for a bid in No trump.

4 Your hand contains 10 points. Count 3 for the K of Hearts, 1 for the J of Clubs, 4 for the A of Diamonds, 1 for the doubleton in Spades, 1 for the doubleton in Diamonds.

5 Your hand contains 7 points. Count 2 for the Q of Spades, 1 for the J of Hearts, 3 for the K of Clubs, 1 for the five-card Heart suit. Do not count anything for the doubleton in Spades. In evaluating your hand for a response to any No trump bid you cannot count points for short suits.

6 Your hand contains 11 points. Count 3 for the K of Clubs, 2 for the Q of Diamonds, 1 for the J of Diamonds, 5 for the void in Spades.

7 Your hand contains 12 points. Count 2 for the Q of Hearts, 3 for the K of Clubs, 4 for the A of Diamonds, 3 for the singleton in Spades.

A2 10 8 6 3 K 5 3 K Q 6 2
♠ ♠ ♡ ♡ ♡ ♡ ♣ ♣ ♣ ♦ ♦ ♦ ♦

8 Your partner opened 1 Spade.
Next player passed.

A 2 K Q J 6 5 10 9 8 J 3 2
♠ ♠ ♡ ♡ ♡ ♡ ♡ ♣ ♣ ♣ ♦ ♦

9 Your partner opened 1 Spade.
Next player passed.

J 10 4 2 8 3 A 6 5 2 10 6 2
♠ ♠ ♠ ♠ ♡ ♡ ♣ ♣ ♣ ♣ ♦ ♦

10 Your partner opened 1 Diamond.
Your right hand opponent passed.

ANSWERS

8 Your hand contains 12 points. Count 4 for the A of Spades, 3 for the K of Clubs, 3 for the K of Diamonds, 2 for the Q of Diamonds. In responding to your partner's opening bid, do not count short suit points for a void, singleton, or doubleton in your partner's suit.

9 Your hand contains 12 points. Count 4 for the A of Spades, 3 for the K of Hearts, 2 for the Q of Hearts, 1 for the J of Hearts, 1 for the J of Diamonds. You cannot count short suit points for a void, singleton, or doubleton in your partner's suit, if you expect the final contract to be in his suit. But in this case, the final contract will probably be in your own Heart suit, so you can count 1 point for the doubleton in your partner's Spade suit.

10 Your hand contains 6 points. Count 1 for the J of Spades, 4 for the A of Clubs, 1 for the doubleton in Hearts. If, however, you are considering a response of 1 No trump you can count only 5 points, because you cannot count points for short suits in evaluating your hand for a bid in No trump.

Lesson 2

TYPE OF HAND

Classified according to distribution

A hand is considered a balanced hand when the cards are almost equally distributed among the 4 suits. The hand must contain no suit shorter than 2 cards, but no more than 1 two-card suit. It must contain no suit longer than 5 cards, but no more than 1 five-card suit.

The length of the suits must be (5-3-3-2) or (4-3-3-3) or (4-4-3-2).

A hand is considered an unbalanced hand unless it contains the exact distribution described above.

Classified according to strength

The strength of a hand depends upon its high cards and also on its distribution. Based on the total number of points a hand contains, it is classified as shown below.

Type of Hand

Opening Bidder	POINTS	Responding Bidder
	6- 9 ..	Minimum*
	10-12 ..	Strong
Minimum	13-15 ..	Very strong
Strong	16-18 ..	Powerful
Very Strong ..	19-21 ..	Tremendous
Powerful	22 & up	

DISTRIBUTION

Balanced Hand—(5-3-3-2) or (4-4-3-2) or (4-3-3-3)
Unbalanced Hand—Any other distribution

* Minimum responding hands are divided into two groups—the lower bracket and the upper bracket.
Hands in the lower bracket contain 6 or 7 points.
Hands in the upper bracket contain 8 or 9 points.

WHAT TYPE OF HAND DO YOU HOLD?

A♠ Q♠ 8♠ 5♠ 2♠ K♥ 9♥ 6♥ Q♣ 10♣ 3♣ 10♦ 9♦

1 You dealt the cards.
It is your opening bid.

A♠ 4♠ K♥ Q♥ J♥ 10♥ 2♥ A♣ 6♣ 5♣ 3♣ K♦ 8♦

2 You dealt the cards.
It is your opening bid.

A♠ 10♠ 2♠ A♥ J♥ 5♥ Q♣ J♣ 3♣ A♦ 9♦ 8♦ 7♦

3 You dealt the cards.
It is your opening bid.

A♠ K♠ J♠ 2♠ A♥ Q♥ J♣ 8♣ 7♣ K♦ Q♦ 9♦ 8♦

4 You dealt the cards.
It is your opening bid.

K♠ 3♠ A♥ J♥ 6♥ 2♥ K♣ Q♣ 8♣ 5♣ J♦ 10♦ 2♦

5 You dealt the cards.
It is your opening bid.

A♠ K♠ Q♠ 5♠ 3♠ 8♥ Q♣ 8♣ 4♣ K♦ Q♦ 8♦ 3♦

6 You dealt the cards.
It is your opening bid.

7 You dealt the cards.
It is your opening bid.

ANSWERS

1 You have a balanced hand. It is not a minimum opening hand, because it contains only 12 points—11 points in high cards and 1 point for the doubleton.

2 You have an unbalanced hand. It is a very strong opening hand, because it contains 19 points—17 points in high cards, 1 point for the doubleton in Spades, and 1 point for the doubleton in Diamonds.

3 You have a balanced hand. It is a strong opening hand, because it contains 16 points in high cards.

4 You have an unbalanced hand. It is a powerful opening hand, because it contains 22 points—20 points in high cards and 2 points for the singleton.

5 You have a balanced hand. It is a minimum opening hand, because it contains 15 points—14 points in high cards and 1 point for the doubleton.

6 You have an unbalanced hand. It is a strong opening hand, because it contains 18 points—16 points in high cards and 2 points for the singleton.

7 You have a balanced hand. It is a very strong opening hand, because it contains 20 points—19 points in high cards and 1 point for the doubleton.

WHAT TYPE OF HAND DO YOU HOLD?

9♠ 5♠ 10♥ 8♥ 6♥ 4♥ 3♥ 8♣ Q♦ 10♦ 7♦ 6♦ 4♦

8 Your partner opened 1 Heart.
   Next player passed.

5♠ 4♠ 10♥ 9♥ 8♥ 5♥ 3♥ A♣ 6♣ A♦ 10♦ 8♦ 6♦

9 Your partner opened 1 Diamond.
   Next player passed.

A♠ K♠ Q♠ 3♠ 6♥ 2♥ K♣ 8♣ 5♣ 6♦ 5♦ 3♦ 2♦

10 Your partner opened 1 Diamond.
   Next player passed.

A♠ K♠ Q♠ 2♠ A♥ 4♥ 3♥ Q♣ 10♣ 3♣ J♦ 9♦ 8♦

11 Your partner opened 1 Heart.
   Next player passed.

K♠ 3♠ A♥ A♣ 8♣ 5♣ 3♣ 2♣ K♦ J♦ 10♦ 8♦ 6♦

12 Your partner opened 1 Club.
   Next player passed.

A	8	4	K	9	7	4	Q	8	6	5	3	2
♠	♠	♠	♥	♥	♥	♥	♣	♣	♣	♦	♦	♦

13 Your partner opened 1 Spade.
Next player passed.

ANSWERS

8 You have an unbalanced hand. It is a minimum responding hand, because it contains 6 points—2 points in high cards, 1 point for the doubleton in Spades, and 3 points for the singleton in Clubs.

9 You have an unbalanced hand. It is a strong responding hand, because it contains 10 points—8 points in high cards, 1 point for the doubleton in Spades, and 1 point for the doubleton in Clubs.

10 You have a balanced hand. It is a very strong responding hand, because it contains 13 points—12 points in high cards, and 1 point for the doubleton.

11 You have a balanced hand. It is a powerful responding hand, because it contains 16 points in high cards.

12 You have an unbalanced hand. It is tremendous responding hand, because it contains 19 points—15 points in high cards, 1 point for the doubleton in Spades, and 3 points for the singleton in Hearts.

13 You have a balanced hand. It is a minimum responding hand, because it contains 9 points in high cards.

WHAT TYPE OF HAND DO YOU HOLD?

A	2	A	5	3	9	7	6	K	8	7	5	2
♠	♠	♡	♡	♡	♣	♣	♣	♦	♦	♦	♦	♦

14 Your partner opened 1 Heart.
Next player passed.

K	J	4	2	A	Q	8	6	4	Q	7	6	5
♠	♠	♠	♠	♡	♣	♣	♣	♣	♦	♦	♦	♦

15 Your partner opened 1 Spade.
Next player passed.

A	8	5	A	K	Q	J	4	2	J	10	8	6
♠	♠	♠	♡	♣	♣	♣	♣	♣	♦	♦	♦	♦

16 Your partner opened 1 Spade.
Next player passed.

ANSWERS

14 You have a balanced hand. It is a strong responding hand, because it contains 12 points—11 points in high cards and 1 point for the doubleton.

15 You have an unbalanced hand. It is a very strong responding hand, because it contains 15 points—12 points in high cards and 3 points for the singleton.

16 You have an unbalanced hand. It is a powerful responding hand, because it contains 18 points—15 points in high cards and 3 points for the singleton.

Lesson 3

TYPE OF SUIT

Depending upon both the length of the suit and the high cards it contains, a suit is classified as follows:

Not biddable

Any 3-card or shorter suit is not biddable.

However, many players occasionally make an opening bid in a 3-card Club suit headed by the Q or better, if no other good opening bid is available.

Any 4 card suit headed Q 9 or less is not biddable.

Do not make an opening bid in a suit not biddable.

Biddable

Any 4-card suit headed A, K, Q 10, or better is biddable.

Note—Some advanced players do not make an opening bid in a four-card major suit, unless it is headed A, KJ, QJ10, or better.

Any 5-card suit is biddable.

Rebid in the same biddable suit only after your partner has raised.

Rebiddable

Any 5-card suit headed AJ, KJ 9, QJ 9, or better is rebiddable.

Any 6-card suit is rebiddable.

Rebid a rebiddable suit once, even if your partner has not raised.

Type of Suit

Biddable

Any 4-card suit headed A, K, Q 10, or better
Any 5-card suit

Rebiddable

Any 5-card suit headed A J, KJ9, QJ9, or better
Any 6-card suit

WHAT TYPE OF SUIT DO YOU HOLD?

1 A♠ K♠ Q♠

2 K♦ 10♦ 6♦ 5♦

3 A♠ 8♠ 7♠ 5♠ 3♠

4 Q♠ J♠ 9♠ 5♠ 2♠

5 J♥ 10♥ 9♥ 8♥

6 A♥ 6♥ 5♥ 4♥

7 K♥ 8♥ 5♥ 4♥ 2♥

8 K♥ J♥ 9♥ 7♥ 4♥

9 Q♣ 9♣ 8♣ 7♣

10 A♣ K♣ Q♣ J♣

11 Q♣ J♣ 5♣ 4♣ 2♣

12 A♣ J♣ 6♣ 5♣ 3♣

13 Q♦ 10♦ 4♦ 2♦

14 8♦ 7♦ 6♦ 5♦ 4♦

15

16 ⟨7⟩⟨6⟩⟨5⟩⟨4⟩⟨3⟩⟨2⟩

ANSWERS

1	Not biddable	9	Not biddable
2	Biddable	10	Biddable
3	Biddable	11	Biddable
4	Rebiddable	12	Rebiddable
5	Not biddable	13	Biddable
6	Biddable	14	Biddable
7	Biddable	15	Biddable
8	Rebiddable	16	Rebiddable

Lesson 4

OPENING BID OF 1 IN A SUIT

If you can count 13 points in your hand, make an opening bid of 1 in a suit, provided you have 1 rebiddable suit or 2 good biddable suits.

Note—In third hand position the requirements for an opening bid are reduced by 1 or 2 points, if the hand contains a strong rebiddable suit.

If you can count 14 points or more, you must always open.

With suits of Unequal length: bid the longest suit first.

Many players occasionally make an opening bid in a 3-card Club suit headed by the Q or better, if no other good opening bid is available.

With suits of Equal length: bid the highest ranking suit first.

With 2 or 3 four-card suits many players open by bidding the suit which ranks just below the shortest suit in the hand.

GOREN'S PRINCIPLE OF PREPAREDNESS

If you open with a bid of 1 in a suit, and your partner responds with a bid in some other suit, you are required to bid at least one more time.

In order to be prepared for your second bid you must have a re-biddable hand. A hand to be rebiddable must contain a rebiddable suit, or 2 good biddable suits, or an excess of points—that is, at least 14 points.

Opening Bid of 1 in a Suit

13 points—Open with 1 rebiddable suit or 2 biddable suits
14 points—Open without fail

With suits of unequal length—Bid the longest suit first
With suits of equal length—Bid the highest ranking suit first

WHAT IS YOUR OPENING BID?

1 A♠ K♠ 10♠ 5♠ 6♥ 4♥ 2♥ 6♣ 3♣ 2♣ A♦ J♦ 6♦

2 A♠ Q♠ 5♠ 4♠ A♥ J♥ 5♥ 2♥ J♣ 8♣ 4♣ 9♦ 6♦

3 A♠ K♠ 8♠ 5♠ 4♠ 7♥ 5♥ 2♥ K♣ 7♣ J♦ 4♦ 3♦

4 A♠ 10♠ 6♠ 5♠ 3♠ A♥ K♥ 2♥ 5♣ 4♣ 3♣ 8♦ 6♦

ANSWERS

1 This hand contains 12 points in high cards. It does not contain the 13 points necessary for an opening bid. Nor does it contain a rebiddable suit or 2 biddable suits. Pass.

2 This hand contains 13 points—12 in high cards and 1 for a doubleton in Diamonds. You have 2 biddable suits. With suits of equal length bid the higher ranking suit first. Open 1 Spade.

3 This hand contains 12 points—11 in high cards and one for a doubleton in Clubs. It has a strong rebiddable suit, but does not contain the 13 points necessary for an opening bid. Pass.

4 This hand contains 12 points—11 in high cards and 1 for a doubleton in Diamonds. It does not contain the 13 points necessary for an opening bid. Pass.

WHAT IS YOUR OPENING BID?

5 A♠ 10♠ 8♠ 6♠ 5♠ A♡ K♡ 8♡ 4♡ 10♣ 9♣ 5◇ 3◇

6 K♠ J♠ 10♠ 6♠ 5♠ 2♠ A♡ 3♡ 8♣ 2♣ Q◇ J◇ 6◇

7 A♠ K♠ 5♠ K♡ 8♡ 3♡ A♣ 9♣ 6♣ 5♣ 6◇ 4◇ 2◇

8 A♠ K♠ 9♠ 7♠ 6♠ 7♡ 5♡ Q♣ J♣ 4♣ 10◇ 9◇ 2◇

9 A♠ K♠ 9♠ 7♠ 6♠ 10♡ 9♡ 4♡ 2♡ 8♣ Q◇ J◇ 4◇

10 A♠ J♠ 6♠ 5♠ 3♠ A♡ K♡ 2♡ 5♣ 4♣ 3♣ 8◇ 6◇

11 K♠ 10♠ 4♠ 2♠ A♡ K♡ Q♡ 2♡ 8♣ 6♣ 4♣ 9◇ 7◇

12 10♠ 9♠ 8♠ 6♠ 4♠ 2♠ K♡ Q♡ 4♡ A♣ Q♣ 3♣ 2♣

ANSWERS

5 This hand contains 13 points—11 in high cards, 1 for the doubleton in Diamonds, and 1 for the doubleton in Clubs. It contains 2 biddable suits. With suits of unequal length bid the longer suit first. Open 1 Spade.

6 This hand contains 13 points—11 in high cards, 1 for the doubleton in Hearts, and 1 for the doubleton in Clubs. You have a rebiddable Spade suit. Open 1 Spade.

7 This hand contains 14 points in high cards. You must make an opening bid even though you have only 1 biddable suit. Open 1 Club.

8 This hand contains 11 points—10 in high cards and 1 for the doubleton in Hearts. Even though you have a strong rebiddable Spade suit, do not open, because you have less than 13 points. Pass.

9 This hand contains 12 points—10 in high cards and 2 for the singleton in Clubs. Your Spade suit is rebiddable. This hand does not contain the 13 points necessary for an opening bid. Pass.

10 This hand contains 13 points—12 in high cards and 1 for the doubleton in Diamonds. Your Spade suit is rebiddable. Open 1 Spade.

11 This hand contains 13 points—12 in high cards and 1 for the doubleton in Diamonds. You have 2 biddable suits. With 2 suits of equal length, bid the higher ranking suit first. Open 1 Spade.

12 This hand contains 14 points—11 in high cards and 3 for the void in Diamonds. Your Spade suit is rebiddable. Open 1 Spade.

Lesson 5

OPENING BID OF 1 NO TRUMP

An opening bid of 1 No trump is made when you have a strong opening hand (16 to 18 points) and a balanced hand as well.

The requirements for an opening bid of 1 No trump are very strict.

You must hold not less than 16 and not more than 18 points in high cards. No points are counted for short suits.

The length of the suits in the hand must be (5-3-3-2) or (4-3-3-3) or (4-4-3-2).

If the hand contains a doubleton, this doubleton must be headed by the K or better.

At least 3 of the suits must contain a stopper such as A, Kx, Qxx, or Jxxx.

With these exact requirements, bid a No trump in preference to a suit. Unless you have these exact requirements, do not bid a No trump.

Opening Bid of 1 No Trump

16 to 18 points in high cards only—No more & no less
Balanced hand—(5-3-3-2) or (4-4-3-2) or (4-3-3-3)
Doubleton—Kx or better
3 suits stopped

WHAT IS YOUR OPENING BID?

1   K 6 4 ♠ A K 8 5 4 ♡ Q J 7 ♣ A 6 ♢

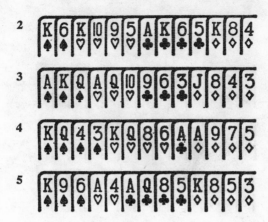

ANSWERS

1 This is a balanced hand. It contains 17 points in high cards. The doubleton is headed by the A. All 4 suits are stopped. Open 1 No trump.

2 This is a balanced hand. It contains 16 points in high cards. The doubleton is headed by the K. All 4 suits are stopped. Open 1 No trump.

3 This is a balanced hand. It contains 16 points in high cards. Three of the suits are stopped. Open 1 No trump.

4 This is an unbalanced hand because it contains a singleton. It contains 18 points in high cards. However, do not bid 1 No trump with an unbalanced hand. Open 1 Spade. With suits of equal length bid the highest ranking suit first.

5 This is a balanced hand. It contains 16 points in high cards. The doubleton is headed by the A. All suits are stopped. Open 1 No trump.

WHAT IS YOUR OPENING BID?

6   K♠ 3♠ A♡ K♡ J♡ 4♡ 8♣ 7♣ 6♣ A♦ 5♦ 3♦ 2♦

7   A♠ K♠ Q♠ 5♠ A♡ 2♡ K♣ Q♣ J♣ 2♣ 9♦ 8♦ 6♦

8   A♠ 8♠ 2♠ A♡ Q♡ 5♡ 4♡ Q♣ 6♣ A♦ 9♦ 8♦ 5♦

9   A♠ 5♠ 4♠ 2♠ A♡ 3♡ A♣ J♣ 8♣ 7♣ 5♣ A♦ 6♦

10   K♠ 9♠ 6♠ A♡ 4♡ A♣ J♣ 8♣ 5♣ 3♣ K♦ 8♦ 5♦

ANSWERS

6 This is a balanced hand. It contains only 15 points in high cards. Do not bid 1 No trump. For an opening bid of 1 No trump 16 points in high cards are required. With 2 suits of equal length bid the higher ranking suit first. Open 1 Heart.

7 This is a balanced hand. It contains 19 points in high cards. You must not make an opening bid of 1 No trump if you hold more than 18 points in high card. With 2 suits of equal length bid the higher ranking suit first. Open 1 Spade.

8 This is a balanced hand. It contains 16 points in high cards. However, do not bid 1 No trump, because the doubleton is not headed by the K or A. With 2 suits of equal length bid the higher ranking suit first. Open 1 Heart.

9 This is an unbalanced hand because it contains two doubletons. It contains 17 points in high cards. However, do not bid 1 No trump with an unbalanced hand. With suits of unequal length bid the longest suit first. Open 1 Club.

10 This is a balanced hand. It contains 16 points—15 points in high cards and 1 for the doubleton in Hearts. Do not open 1 No trump with less than 16 points in high cards. Open 1 Club.

Lesson 6

SUIT TAKE-OUT
IN RESPONSE TO OPENING BID OF 1 IN A SUIT

When your partner has made an opening bid of 1 in a suit, and you have a biddable suit of your own, if possible show your partner where your strength lies by responding with a bid in your own suit.

When you respond by bidding at the level of 1 in a higher ranking suit than your partner's, you make a "one over one" take-out.

A *"one over one" response* requires at least a minimum responding hand (6 to 9 points).

When you respond by bidding at the level of 2 in a lower ranking suit than your partner's, you make a "two over one" take-out.

A *"two over one" response* requires at least a strong responding hand (10 to 12 points).

Neither the "one over one" nor the "two over one" is a limited bid. These responses can also be made when you have stronger responding hands.

A response of "one over one" or "two over one" is an encouraging response. It forces your partner to keep the bidding open for at least one round.

A "one over one" or "two over one" is usually preferred to a single raise in partner's suit or to a response of 1 No trump.

Response to Opening Bid of 1 In a Suit

Suit Take-out

One over one— 6 to 9 points —With a biddable suit
Two over one—10 to 12 points —With a biddable suit

34

WHAT IS YOUR BID?

1 Your partner opened 1 Heart.
Next player passed.

2 Your partner opened 1 Heart.
Next player passed.

3 Your partner opened 1 Diamond.
Next player passed.

ANSWERS

1 This hand contains 6 points—5 in high cards and 1 for the doubleton in Hearts. You cannot make a "one over one" response because your Spade suit is not biddable. You cannot make a "two over one" response because you have less than 10 points. You cannot respond 1 No trump because you have only 5 points in high cards. Therefore, pass.

2 This hand contains 6 points—5 in high cards and 1 for the doubleton in Hearts. Your Spade suit is biddable. Respond 1 Spade.

3 This hand contains 8 points—7 in high cards and 1 for the doubleton in Clubs. Your Heart suit is biddable. Respond 1 Heart.

WHAT IS YOUR BID?

4 Your partner opened 1 Spade.
Next player passed.

5 Your partner opened 1 Heart.
Next player passed.

6 Your partner opened 1 Spade.
Next player passed.

7 Your partner opened 1 Diamond.
Next player passed.

8 Your partner opened 1 Diamond.
Next player passed.

ANSWERS

4 This hand contains 10 points—7 in high cards, 2 for the singleton in Spades, and 1 for the doubleton in Clubs. Your Diamond suit is rebiddable. Respond 2 Diamonds.

5 This hand contains 11 points—10 in high cards and 1 for the doubleton in Spades. Your Diamond suit is biddable. Respond 2 Diamonds.

6 This hand contains 10 points—9 in high cards and 1 for the doubleton in Clubs. Your Heart suit is rebiddable. Respond 2 Hearts.

7 This hand contains 6 points—5 in high cards and 1 for the doubleton in Clubs. Your Heart suit is biddable. Respond 1 Heart.

8 This hand contains 6 points—5 in high cards and 1 for the doubleton in Spades. You cannot respond 1 Heart because your Heart suit is not biddable. You cannot respond 2 Clubs because you do not have 10 points. You cannot respond 1 No trump because you have less than 6 points in high cards. Therefore, pass.

Lesson 7

RAISING PARTNER'S OPENING BID
OF 1 IN A SUIT

In order to raise your partner's bid of 1 in a suit (to bid the same suit at a higher level), you must always have adequate length in trumps.

Without adequate length in trumps, you must not raise your partner's suit no matter how many high card points you hold. A single raise requires 4 small trumps, or 3 trumps headed by Q or J 10. After your partner has rebid his suit, 1 less trump is required.

If you know that your partner occasionally makes an opening bid in a 3-card Club suit, do not raise his opening bid of 1 Club, if you hold less than 4 Clubs.

When you consider raising partner's suit, remember you can count 1 point for a doubleton, 3 for a singleton, and 5 for a void.

To make a single raise you must have not only support for your partner in trumps, but also a minimum responding hand (6 to 9 points). A single raise is limited to hands of this class. If you have 10 points or more, you should make some other response.

Some advanced players will not give a single raise with less than 7 points.

A single raise is a weak or discouraging response. It does not force your partner to keep the bidding open even for one round. Do not respond with a single raise if you have the requirements for a response of "one over one" or "two over one."

A double raise (from one to three) shows both length in trumps and strength in points. A double raise should not be given unless you have a very strong responding hand (13 to 15 points), including 5 small trumps or 4 trumps headed by the Q or J 10.

A double raise forces your partner to keep the bidding open until the game is reached.

A triple raise (from one to four) shows great length in trumps, but weakness in points.

At least 5 trumps must be held.

The hand must contain a singleton or void.

A triple raise should not be given if the hand meets the requirements for a double raise. It should not be given if the hand contains more than 9 points in high cards.

It should be made only in a major suit.

Response to Opening Bid of 1 in a Suit

Single Raise in Partner's Suit

6 to 9 points—With x x x x, Q x x, or J 10 x in trump suit

WHAT IS YOUR RESPONSE?

1 Your partner opened 1 Heart.
Next player passed.

ANSWER

1 This hand contains 7 points—4 in high cards and 3 for the singleton in Spades. You have adequate trump support. Raise to 2 Hearts.

WHAT IS YOUR RESPONSE?

2 Your partner opened 1 Heart.
Next player passed.

3 Your partner opened 1 Spade.
Next player passed.

4 Your partner opened 1 Heart.
Next player passed.

5 Your partner opened 1 Heart.
Next player passed.

6 Your partner opened 1 Spade.
Next player passed.

ANSWERS

2 This hand contains 6 points—5 in high cards and 1 for the doubleton in Spades. You have adequate trump support. Raise to 2 Hearts.

3 This hand contains 7 points in high cards. You have adequate trump support. Raise to 2 Spades.

4 This hand contains 12 points—7 in high cards, 5 for the void in Spades. You have adequate trump support. However, you must not respond with a single raise if you have 10 points or more. Respond 2 Diamonds.

5 This hand contains 5 points—4 in high cards and 1 for the doubleton in Spades. You have adequate trump support. However, you cannot raise your partner's suit without 6 points. You cannot bid 2 Diamonds without 10 points. You cannot bid 1 No trump without 6 points in high cards. Therefore, pass.

6 This hand contains 6 points—5 in high cards and 1 for the doubleton in Clubs. You cannot raise your partner's suit because you do not have adequate trump support. You cannot respond 2 Hearts because you do not have 10 points. You cannot bid 1 No trump because you do not have 6 points in high cards. Therefore, pass.

Lesson 8

NO TRUMP TAKE-OUT
IN RESPONSE TO OPENING BID OF 1 IN A SUIT

When your partner has made an opening bid of 1 in a suit, you may be able to keep the bidding open, even though you do not have the requirements to respond with a "one over one," or a "two over one," or a single raise in your partner's suit.

Even though you do not have a biddable suit of your own or adequate trump support for your partner, you may still respond by bidding 1 No trump, if you have a minimum responding hand (6 to 9 points).

In valuing your hand for a response of 1 No trump do not count points for doubletons, singletons or voids. No points are counted for short suits for any kind of No trump bid.

A response of 1 No trump is limited to minimum responding hands (6 to 9 points). If you have 10 points or more (counting points both for high cards and short suits), you should make some other response.

Advanced players sometimes respond 1 No trump with 10 points, when no other good response is available.

A response of I No trump is a weak or discouraging response. It does not force your partner to keep the bidding open even for one round. Do not make a response of 1 No trump, if you have the requirements for a response of "one over one," or "two over one," or a raise in your partner's suit.

Response to Opening Bid of 1 In A Suit

Take-out of 1 No trump

6 to 9 points—in high cards only—No more & no less

WHAT IS YOUR RESPONSE?

1 Your partner opened 1 Heart.
Next player passed.

2 Your partner opened 1 Heart.
Next player passed.

ANSWERS

1 This hand contains 6 points—5 in high cards and 1 for the doubleton in Hearts. Do not raise your partner's Heart suit because you do not have adequate trump support. Do not respond 1 No trump because you do not have 6 points in high cards. Therefore, pass.

2 This hand contains 7 points—6 in high cards and 1 for the doubleton in Hearts. Do not raise your partner's Heart suit because you do not have adequate trump support. Do not respond 2 Diamonds because you do not have 10 points. With 6 points in high cards, respond 1 No trump.

WHAT IS YOUR RESPONSE?

3 Your partner opened 1 Diamond.
Next player passed.

4 Your partner opened 1 Spade.
Next player passed.

5 Your partner opened 1 Spade.
Next player passed.

6 Your partner opened 1 Spade.
Next player passed.

ANSWERS

3 This hand contains 6 points—5 in high cards and 1 for the doubleton in Clubs. You cannot respond 1 No trump but you can make a "one over one" response. You have a biddable Heart suit and 6 points. Therefore, respond 1 Heart.

4 This hand contains 8 points—7 in high cards and 1 for the doubleton in Diamonds. Do not raise your partner's Spade suit because you do not have adequate trump support. Do not respond 2 Hearts because you do not have 10 points. With 6 points in high cards, respond 1 No trump.

5 This hand contains 9 points in high cards. Do not raise your partner's Spade suit because you do not have adequate trump support. Do not respond 2 Hearts because you do not have 10 points. With 6 points in high cards, respond 1 No trump.

6 This hand contains 10 points in high cards. Do not respond 1 No trump because you have more than 9 points in high cards. Do not raise your partner's Spade suit because you do not have adequate trump support and you have more than 9 points. With 10 points and a biddable Heart suit, respond 2 Hearts.

Lesson 9

FORCING RESPONSES
TO OPENING BID OF 1 IN A SUIT

When the opening bidder makes a bid of 1 in a suit, his hand probably contains 13 points or more. Therefore, if the partner of the opening bidder also holds 13 points, the two hands together probably contain 26 points or more.

When you and your partner together hold 26 points, you can almost always make a game, if you can find the right contract.

When your partner makes an opening bid, and you have a very strong responding hand (13 to 15 points), force your partner to keep the bidding open until game is reached.

Any jump response of 1 trick more than is required to keep the bidding open is forcing to game.

A jump response of 2 No trump requires a very strong responding hand (13 to 15 points), a balanced hand, and a stopper in all unbid suits.

A jump response of 3 No trump requires a powerful responding hand (16 to 18 points), distribution (4-3-3-3), and a stopper in all unbid suits.

A double raise in your partner's suit (a jump from 1 to 3 in his suit) requires a very strong responding hand (13 to 15 points), and it also requires at least 4 trumps.

A jump response in a new suit requires a tremendous hand (19 to 21 points). A jump in a new suit should rarely be made unless you have a long, strong suit, or four card support for partner's suit.

A jump in a new suit is an invitation to try for a slam.

Response to Opening Bid of 1 in a Suit

Jump to 2 No Trump

13 to 15 points—With balanced hand & stopper in all unbid suits

Jump to 3 in Partner's Suit

13 to 15 points—With x x x x in trump suit

Jump in a New Suit

19 to 21 points—With long strong suit, or
With 4 of partner's suit

WHAT IS YOUR RESPONSE?

1 Your partner opened 1 Heart.
Next player passed.

2 Your partner opened 1 Spade.
Next player passed.

ANSWERS

1 This hand contains 13 points in high cards. It is a balanced hand with strength in all the suits not bid by your partner. Jump to 2 No trump.

2 This hand contains 13 points—10 in high cards and 3 for the singleton in Hearts. You have 1 Spade more than required for a single raise. Jump to 3 Spades.

WHAT IS YOUR RESPONSE?

3 Your partner opened 1 Diamond.
Next player passed.

4 Your partner opened 1 Heart.
Next player passed.

5 Your partner opened 1 Diamond.
Next player passed.

6 Your partner opened 1 Heart.
Next player passed.

7 Your partner opened 1 Spade.
Next player passed.

8 Your partner opened 1 Heart.
Next player passed.

ANSWERS

3 This hand contains 19 points—16 in high cards, 2 for the singleton in Spades, and 1 for the doubleton in Diamonds. You have a long, strong Heart suit. Jump to 2 Hearts.

4 This hand contains 20 points—17 in high cards and 3 for the singleton in Spades. You have 1 Heart more than required for a single raise. Do not respond 3 Hearts. If you hold 16 points or more your hand is too strong for a double raise. With 19 points or more and 4-card support for your partner's suit, jump in a new suit, even though it is not a long, strong suit. Therefore, jump to 3 Diamonds.

5 This hand contains 13 points in high cards. It is a balanced hand. Do not jump to 2 No trump. You do not have strength in Hearts. Respond 2 Clubs.

6 This hand contains 14 points—13 in high cards and 1 for the doubleton in Clubs. You have 1 Heart more than required for a single raise. Jump to 3 Hearts.

7 This hand contains 12 points in high cards. It is a balanced hand with strength in all the suits not bid by your partner. However, do not jump to 2 No trump, unless you have 13 points in high cards. Respond 2 Hearts.

8 This hand contains 13 points—12 in high cards and 1 for the doubleton in Diamonds. Do not jump to 3 Hearts. You do not have 1 Heart more than required for a single raise. Respond 1 Spade.

WHAT IS YOUR RESPONSE?

A♠ J♠ 9♠ 2♠ A♡ 10♡ 9♡ 7♡ 5♡ 8♣ 10♦ 7♦ 5♦

9 Your partner opened 1 Heart.
Next player passed.

ANSWERS

9 This hand contains 12 points—9 in high cards and 3 for the singleton in Clubs. You have 2 Hearts more than required for a single raise. Do not jump to 3 hearts if you have less than 13 points. Do not give a single raise if you have more than 9 points. Respond 1 Spade.

Lesson 10

RESPONSE TO OPENING BID OF 1 NO TRUMP

In valuing a hand for a response to an opening bid of 1 No trump, do not count points for short suits. However, add 1 extra point to your count if your hand contains a five-card or longer suit.

Bear in mind that at a No trump contract with 26 points in the combined hands you can make a game; with 33, a small slam; and with 37, a grand slam.

Bear in mind also that your partner holds 16, 17, or 18 points in high cards.

With a worthless responding hand (less than 6 points)

Pass, or bid 2 in a suit if you have a six or seven card Spade, Heart, or Diamond suit in which the hand can be safely played at a low level. Do not bid a Club suit.*

With a minimum responding hand (6 to 9 points)

If your hand is in the lower bracket (6 or 7 points)
With a balanced hand—Pass
With an unbalanced hand—Bid 2 in a suit, if you have a good five-card Spade, Heart, or Diamond suit. Do not bid a Club suit.* Jump to 4 in a suit if you have a six or seven card major suit.

A response of 2 in a suit is a discouraging response. It shows your partner that the combined hands do not contain 26 points in high cards.

If your hand is in the upper bracket (8 or 9 points)
Bid 2 No trump; or jump to 4 in a suit if you have a six or seven card major suit. Do not bid 2 in a suit.

A response of 2 No trump is an encouraging response. It invites your partner to go on to game, if he holds more than a minimum opening No trump hand.

---

* Some advanced players respond 2 Clubs (an artificial bid) to show a hand with 8 or 9 points or more that contains a four-card or longer major suit. This is known as the Stayman Convention.

With a strong responding hand (10 to 12 points), or with a very strong responding hand (13 to 15 points)

Jump to 3 No trump, or jump to 3 in a suit if you have a six card or a strong five card suit. A jump to 3 in a suit is forcing to game.

With a powerful hand (16 to 18) points

If you have only 16 points—Bid 4 No trump.
If you have 17 or 18 points—Bid 6 No trump.

After an opening bid of 1 No trump, a bid of 4 No trump invites your partner to jump directly to a slam. A 4 No trump bid in this case is not the Blackwood Convention asking your partner to tell you how many aces he holds.

Response to Opening Bid of 1 No Trump

0 to 5 points		Pass, or Bid 2 in long safe suit
6 to 9 points	With 6 to 7 points	Pass, or Bid 2 in 5-card suit, or Bid 4 in 6-card major
	With 8 to 9 points	Bid 2 No trump, or Bid 4 in 6-card major
10 to 12 points 13 to 15 points		Bid 3 No trump, or Bid 3 in long strong suit
16 to 18 points	With only 16 points	Bid 4 No trump
	With 17 or 18 points	Bid 6 No trump, or Bid 6 in long strong suit

WHAT IS YOUR RESPONSE?

Your Partner Opened 1 No trump. Next Player Passed.

1 K♠ J♠ 8♠ 5♠ 4♠ 7♥ 5♥ 2♥ J♣ 7♣ 9♦ 4♦ 3♦

2 A♠ K♠ 8♠ 5♠ 3♥ 9♥ 2♥ 10♣ 5♣ 2♣ 6♦ 5♦ 3♦

3 K♠ 6♠ K♥ 10♥ 5♥ 3♥ K♣ 8♣ 3♣ Q♦ 9♦ 4♦ 2♦

ANSWERS

1 This hand contains 6 points—5 in high cards and 1 for the 5-card Spade suit. With 6 or 7 points and a 5-card suit (other than Clubs), respond by bidding 2 in the suit. Respond 2 Spades.

2 This hand contains 8 points—7 in high cards and 1 for the 5-card Spade suit. Do not bid 2 Spades. With 8 points, respond 2 No trump.

However, if you know that your partner is an advanced player and that he uses the 2 Club Convention, respond 2 Clubs to show that your hand contains 8 or more points and a 4 card or longer major suit.

3 This is a balanced hand. It contains 11 points in high cards. With 11 points and a balanced hand, respond 3 No trump.

However, if you know that your partner is an advanced player and that he uses the Stayman Convention, respond 2 Clubs to show that your hand contains 8 or more points and a 4 card or longer major suit.

WHAT IS YOUR RESPONSE?

Your Partner Opened 1 No trump. Next Player Passed.

4 K♠ Q♠ 9♠ 8♠ 7♠ 3♠ 8♥ 8♣ 7♦ 8♦ 5♦ 3♦ 2♦

5 K♠ 8♠ 7♠ 6♠ 5♠ A♥ 8♥ 6♥ 4♥ 8♣ 7♣ 6♣ 9♦

6 Q♠ 8♠ 6♠ 3♠ 5♥ 4♥ 9♣ A♦ K♦ J♦ 6♦ 5♦ 2♦

7 9♥ 8♥ 6♥ 10♣ 5♣ 3♣ Q♦ 10♦ 9♦ 7♦ 5♦ 3♦ 2♦

8 K♠ 8♠ 3♠ Q♥ 7♥ 6♥ J♣ 4♣ 2♣ J♦ 8♦ 5♦ 3♦

9 8♠ 7♠ K♥ 8♥ 7♥ 6♥ 5♥ 3♥ 9♣ 4♣ A♦ 8♦ 6♦

10 K♠ 9♠ 6♠ A♥ 4♥ A♣ Q♣ 8♣ 5♣ K♦ 8♦ 5♦ 3♦

ANSWERS

4 This hand contains 6 points—5 in high cards, and 1 for the 6-card Spade suit. With 6 or 7 points and a 6-card or longer Spade suit, respond 4 Spades.

5 This hand contains 8 points—7 in high cards and 1 for the 5-card Spade suit. With 8 points, respond 2 No trump.

However, if you know that your partner is an advanced player and that he uses the Stayman Convention, respond 2 Clubs to show that your hand contains 8 or more points and a 4 card or longer major suit.

6 This is an unbalanced hand. It contains 11 points—10 in high cards, and 1 for the 6-card Diamond suit. With 10 points and a long, strong suit, jump to 3 in the suit in preference to bidding 3 No trump. Respond 3 Diamonds.

7 This is an unbalanced hand. It contains 3 points—2 in high cards and 1 for the 7-card Diamond suit. With this hand, the only safe contract is a Diamond contract at a low level. Respond 2 Diamonds.

8 This hand contains 7 points in high cards. With less than 8 points and no 5-card or longer suit, pass.

9 This hand contains 8 points—7 in high cards and 1 for the 6-card Heart suit. With 8 or 9 points and a 6 or 7-card major suit, jump to 4 in the major suit. Respond 4 Hearts.

10 This hand contains 16 points in high cards. With 16 points, jump to 4 No trump.

Lesson 11

REBID BY OPENING BIDDER
AFTER ORIGINAL OPENING BID OF 1 NO TRUMP

When partner responds with 2 in a suit

When you have opened with 1 No trump and your partner has responded with 2 in a suit, you know that he has less than 8 points. Usually after this discouraging response you should pass.

If, however, you have the maximum holding for an opening No trump bid (18 points) and also have strong trump support for your partner's suit, there may still be a remote chance to make a game. In this case raise your partner's suit to 3. Do not make any other rebid.

When partner responds with 3 in a suit

If your partner has made a jump response by bidding 3 in a suit, you are forced to keep the bidding open until game is reached.

When partner responds with 2 No trump

When you have opened with 1 No trump and your partner has responded with 2 No trump, you know that he has 8 or 9 points. His response is encouraging. Therefore rebid, unless you have only the minimum holding for an opening No trump bid (16 points).

When partner responds with 4 No trump

If you have only 16 points—Pass.
If you have 17 or 18 points—Bid 6 No trump.

When you have opened the bidding with 1 No trump, pass instead of rebidding:

1—When your partner responds 3 No trump or 4 in a major.

2—When your partner responds 2 No trump and you have only 16 points (a minimum opening No trump hand).

3—When your partner responds 2 in a suit, unless you have 18 points (a maximum opening No trump hand) and also strong support for your partner's suit.

When you have opened the bidding with 1 No trump, if your partner responds 2 Clubs and he is an advanced player who uses the Stayman Convention, rebid as follows:

2 Diamonds, if your hand contains no four-card major suit.

2 Hearts, if your hand contains a four-card Heart suit.

2 Spades, if your hand contains a four-card Spade suit.

2 Spades, if your hands contains both a four-card Spade suit and a four-card Heart suit.

Rebid by Opening Bidder

AFTER ORIGINAL OPENING BID OF 1 NO TRUMP

When Partner Responds 2 in a Suit

Less than 18 points		Pass
18 points..	A maximum No trump & Strong trump support	Raise Partner

When Partner Responds 2 No Trump

16 points..A minimum No trump..		Pass
More than 16 points		Rebid

When Partner Responds 4 No Trump

16 points..A minimum No trump..		Pass
More than 16 points		Bid 6 No trump

WHAT IS YOUR REBID?

| Q | J | 7 | K | Q | 3 | 2 | A | K | 4 | K | 7 | 3 |
| ♠ | ♠ | ♠ | ♥ | ♥ | ♥ | ♥ | ♣ | ♣ | ♣ | ♦ | ♦ | ♦ |

1   You opened 1 No trump.
    Your partner responded 2 Diamonds.
    Your opponents did not bid.

| A | K | Q | A | Q | 10 | 9 | 6 | 2 | J | 8 | 4 | 3 |
| ♠ | ♠ | ♠ | ♥ | ♥ | ♥ | ♣ | ♣ | ♣ | ♦ | ♦ | ♦ | ♦ |

2   You opened 1 No trump.
    Your partner responded 2 No trump.
    Your opponents did not bid.

| A | J | 3 | K | Q | 10 | 3 | Q | J | 3 | 2 | A | 5 |
| ♠ | ♠ | ♠ | ♥ | ♥ | ♥ | ♥ | ♣ | ♣ | ♣ | ♣ | ♦ | ♦ |

3   You opened 1 No trump.
    Your partner responded 2 No trump.
    Your opponents did not bid.

| A | J | 3 | K | Q | 10 | Q | J | 3 | 2 | A | 5 | 4 |
| ♠ | ♠ | ♠ | ♥ | ♥ | ♥ | ♣ | ♣ | ♣ | ♣ | ♦ | ♦ | ♦ |

4   You opened 1 No trump.
    Your partner responded 2 No trump.
    Your opponents did not bid.

| 8 | 4 | 3 | K | Q | 8 | A | K | 3 | A | 5 | 4 | 2 |
| ♠ | ♠ | ♠ | ♥ | ♥ | ♥ | ♣ | ♣ | ♣ | ♦ | ♦ | ♦ | ♦ |

5   You opened 1 No trump.
    Your partner responded 2 No trump.
    Your opponents did not bid.

8♠ 7♠ 6♠ 4♠ A♥ K♥ 3♥ A♣ 8♣ 6♣ A♦ Q♦ 3♦

6 You opened 1 No trump.
Your partner responded 2 Spades.
Your opponents did not bid.

ANSWERS

1 This hand contains 18 points in high cards. When your partner responds 2 in a suit, do not rebid unless you have 18 points (which is a maximum opening No trump hand) and also have strong trump support for your partner's suit. You have only minimum trump support for your partner's Diamond suit. Therefore, pass.

2 This hand contains 16 points in high cards. When your partner responds 2 No trump, do not rebid if you have only 16 points, which is a minimum opening No trump hand. Pass.

3 This hand contains 17 points in high cards. When your partner responds 2 No trump, rebid if you have more than 16 points—more than a minimum No trump hand. If you have a 4-card major suit, bid 3 in a major suit in preference to 3 No trump. Bid 3 Hearts.

4 This hand contains 17 points in high cards. When your partner responds 2 No trump, rebid if you have more than 16 points—more than a minimum No trump hand. Since you do not have a 4-card major suit, bid 3 No trump.

5 This hand contains 16 points in high cards. When your partner responds 2 No trump, pass if your hand contains only 16 points. Pass.

6 This hand contains 17 points in high cards. When your partner responds 2 in a suit, do not rebid if you have less than 18 points in high cards, even though you have 4-card trump support for your partner's suit. Pass.

WHAT IS YOUR REBID?

A♠ Q♠ 4♠ K♥ Q♥ 2♥ A♣ 10♣ 8♣ 4♣ Q♦ 10♦ 2♦

7 You opened 1 No trump.
Your partner responded 2 Spades.
Your opponents did not bid.

Q♠ 10♠ 3♠ A♥ K♥ 4♥ K♣ Q♣ 8♣ 6♣ 5♣ K♦ 5♦

8 You opened 1 No trump.
Your partner responded 2 Spades.
Your opponents did not bid.

K♠ Q♠ 10♠ 2♠ Q♥ 8♥ 3♥ A♣ Q♣ 2♣ A♦ 8♦ 6♦

9 You opened 1 No trump.
Your partner responded 2 Hearts.
Your opponents did not bid.

K♠ 6♠ K♥ J♥ 10♥ 5♥ A♣ Q♣ 6♣ 5♣ K♦ Q♦ 4♦

10 You opened 1 No trump.
Your partner responded 2 Diamonds.
Your opponents did not bid.

K♠ 9♠ 6♠ A♥ 4♥ A♣ Q♣ 8♣ 5♣ K♦ 8♦ 5♦ 3♦

11 You opened 1 No trump.
Your partner responded 4 No trump.
Your opponents did not bid.

ANSWERS

7 This hand contains 17 points in high cards. When your partner responds 2 in a suit, do not rebid if you have less than 18 points. Do not raise your partner's suit even though you hold 3 of his suit, including 2 of the 3 top honors. Pass.

8 This hand contains 17 points in high cards. When your partner responds 2 in a suit, do not rebid, unless you have 18 points and also have strong trump support for your partner's suit. Pass.

9 This hand contains 17 points in high cards. When your partner responds 2 in a suit, do not rebid unless your hand contains 18 points and also contains strong trump support for your partner's suit. Pass.

10 This hand contains 18 points in high cards. When your partner responds 2 in a suit, rebid if you have 18 points and also have strong trump support for your partner's suit. Raise to 3 Diamonds.

11 This hand contains 16 points in high cards. When your partner responds 4 No trump, do not try to slam if you have only 16 points. Pass.

Lesson 12

REBID BY OPENING BIDDER
AFTER ORIGINAL BID OF 1 IN A SUIT

When partner responds with 1 No trump

After you have opened the bidding with 1 in a suit, if your partner responds with 1 No trump, his bid is the weakest, most discouraging response he can make. It is not forcing even for one round.

In this case, you cannot count on your partner for more than 6 points.

With a minimum hand (13 to 15 points) or
With a strong hand (16 to 18 points)

If you have a balanced hand, pass.
If you have an unbalanced hand, rebid only for safety.
When your hand is not suited for a No trump contract, you may find it safer to rebid, if you have a strong rebiddable suit, or if you have 2 good five-card suits.

With a very strong hand (19 to 21 points)

If you have a balanced hand, jump to 3 No trump.
If you have an unbalanced hand, jump to game in your suit, or game in No trump, or jump in a new suit provided it is a strong suit.

A jump rebid in a new suit forces your partner to keep the bidding open until game is reached.

Rebid By Opening Bidder

AFTER ORIGINAL BID OF 1 IN A SUIT

When Partner Responds with 1 No trump

13 to 15 points
16 to 18 points ..Pass or make a weak rebid for safety

19 to 21 points ..Jump

WHAT IS YOUR REBID?

K8 6 AKJ 5 2 Q6 4 6 4
♠ ♠ ♠ ♥ ♥ ♥ ♥ ♥ ♣ ♣ ♣ ♦ ♦

1 You opened 1 Heart
Your partner responded 1 No trump.
Your opponents did not bid.

AQJ 3 10 8 7 4 2 AQ J 2
♠ ♠ ♠ ♠ ♥ ♥ ♥ ♣ ♣ ♣ ♦ ♦ ♦

2 You opened 1 Spade.
Your partner responded 1 No trump.
Your opponents did not bid.

ANSWERS

1 This hand contains 14 points—13 in high cards and 1 for the doubleton in Diamonds. It is a balanced hand. Do not rebid your Hearts. It is not necessary to do so for safety. With a minimum opening hand (13 to 15 points) which is balanced, pass.

2 This hand contains 15 points—14 in high cards and 1 for the doubleton in Hearts. It is a balanced hand. Do not rebid in Diamonds. It is not necessary to do so for safety. With a minimum opening hand (13 to 15 points) which is balanced, pass.

WHAT IS YOUR REBID?

A♠ J♠ 10♠ 7♠ 5♠ 3♠ K♥ 8♥ 5♥ Q♣ 8♣ 5♣ 6♦

3 You opened 1 Spade.
Your partner responded 1 No trump.
Your opponents did not bid.

A♠ J♠ 9♠ 5♠ 4♠ K♥ 2♥ 7♥ A♦ 10♦ 9♦ 5♦ 3♦

4 You opened 1 Spade.
Your partner responded 1 No trump.
Your opponents did not bid.

A♠ K♠ 7♠ 4♠ Q♥ 5♥ 3♥ 8♣ 7♣ A♦ K♦ 5♦ 3♦

5 You opened 1 Spade.
Your partner responded 1 No trump.
Your opponents did not bid.

K♠ 3♠ A♥ K♥ 8♥ 7♥ A♣ Q♣ 4♣ A♦ 10♦ 8♦ 2♦

6 You opened 1 Heart.
Your partner responded 1 No trump.
Your opponents did not bid.

A♠ K♠ J♠ 9♠ 7♠ 5♠ A♥ J♥ 3♥ K♣ J♣ 3♣ 9♦

7 You opened 1 Spade.
Your partner responded 1 No trump.
Your opponents did not bid.

8 You opened 1 Spade.
Your partner responded 1 No trump.
Your opponents did not bid.

ANSWERS

3 This hand contains 12 points—10 in high cards and 2 for the singleton in Diamonds. It is an unbalanced hand. With a minimum opening hand (13 to 15 points) which is unbalanced, if you have a strong rebiddable suit, rebid for safety. Bid 2 Spades.

4 This hand contains 15 points—12 in high cards, 1 for the doubleton in Hearts, and 2 for the singleton in Clubs. It is an unbalanced hand. With a minimum opening hand (13 to 15 points) which is unbalanced, if you have 2 good 5-card suits, rebid for safety. Bid 2 Diamonds.

5 This hand contains 17 points—16 in high cards and 1 for the doubleton in Clubs. It is a balanced hand. Do not rebid in Diamonds. It is not necessary to do so for safety. With a strong opening hand (16 to 18 points) which is balanced, pass.

6 This hand contains 20 points in high cards. It is a balanced hand. With a very strong opening hand (19 to 21 points), jump to game. With a balanced hand, bid 3 No trump.

7 This hand contains 19 points—17 in high cards and 2 for the singleton in Diamonds. It is an unbalanced hand. With a very strong opening hand (19 to 21 points), jump to game. Bid 4 Spades.

8 This hand contains 19 points—16 in high cards, 1 for the doubleton in Clubs, and 2 for the singleton in Diamonds. It is an unbalanced hand. With a very strong opening hand (19 to 21 points) and 2 strong suits, jump in a new suit. Bid 3 Hearts.

Lesson 13

REBID BY OPENING BIDDER

AFTER ORIGINAL BID OF 1 IN A SUIT

When partner responds with a single raise

When your partner responds with a single raise in your suit, he makes a discouraging response. A single raise is not forcing even for one round.

In this case you cannot count on your partner for more than 6 points.

Before deciding on a rebid, you must revalue your hand. Because your partner has support for your trump suit, the value of the small trumps in your own hand is increased. Therefore count:

1 extra point for your 5th trump.
2 extra points for your 6th trump.
2 extra points for your 7th trump, etc.

With a minimum hand (13 to 15 points)

Pass if the revalued hand is a minimum hand.

With a strong hand (16 to 18 points)

Rebid if the revalued hand is a strong hand.

Bid 3 in your original suit, or 3 in a suit lower ranking than the suit in which you opened the bidding, or 2 in a higher ranking suit. Don't jump.

With a very strong hand (19 to 21 points)

Jump if your revalued hand is a very strong hand.

Jump to game in your suit, or game in No trump, or jump in a new suit.

A jump rebid in a new suit forces your partner to keep the bidding open until game is reached.

Rebid By Opening Bidder

AFTER ORIGINAL BID OF 1 IN A SUIT

When Partner Responds with a Single Raise

13 to 15 points— Pass
16 to 18 points— Rebid
19 to 21 points— Jump

WHAT IS YOUR REBID?

1   You opened 1 Spade.
    Your partner responded 2 Spades.
    Your opponents did not bid.

ANSWERS

1   For an opening bid this hand contains 14 points—13 in
high cards and 1 for the doubleton in Diamonds. After
your partner has raised your suit, you can count 1 additional point for your fifth Spade. So your revalued hand
contains 15 points. When your partner gives you a single
raise, if your revalued hand is a minimum opening hand
(13 to 15 points), do not rebid. Pass.

WHAT IS YOUR REBID?

A♠ Q♠ J♠ 8♠ 4♠ K♥ J♥ 2♥ 10♣ 7♣ Q♦ J♦ 8♦

2 You opened 1 Spade.
Your partner responded 2 Spades.
Your opponents did not bid.

A♠ Q♠ J♠ 8♠ 4♠ 3♥ 9♥ 8♥ 6♣ 4♣ K♦ J♦ 2♦

3 You opened 1 Spade.
Your partner responded 2 Spades.
Your opponents did not bid.

A♠ K♠ 9♠ 7♠ 6♠ 5♥ A♥ 7♣ 3♣ K♦ J♦ 10♦ 2♦

4 You opened 1 Spade.
Your partner responded 2 Spades.
Your opponents did not bid.

A♠ K♠ 9♠ 7♠ Q♥ 5♥ J♣ 10♣ 8♣ 5♣ A♦ Q♦ 6♦

5 You opened 1 Spade.
Your partner responded 2 Spades.
Your opponents did not bid.

A♠ K♠ Q♠ 8♠ 4♠ 8♥ K♣ 3♣ 2♣ A♦ 10♦ 9♦ 3♦

6 You opened 1 Spade.
Your partner responded 2 Spades.
Your opponents did not bid.

ANSWERS

2 For an opening bid this hand contains 15 points—14 in high cards and 1 for the doubleton in Clubs. After your partner has raised your suit, you can count 1 additional point for your fifth Spade. So your revalued hand contains 16 points. When your partner gives you a single raise, if your revalued hand is a strong opening hand (16 to 18 points), rebid. Bid 3 Spades.

3 For an opening bid this hand contains 13 points—11 in high cards, 1 for the doubleton in Hearts, and 1 for the doubleton in Clubs. After your partner has raised your suit, you can count 1 additional point for your fifth Spade and 2 additional points for your sixth Spade. So your revalued hand contains 16 points. When your partner gives you a single raise, if your revalued hand is a strong opening hand (16 to 18 points), rebid. Bid 3 Spades.

4 This hand contains 16 points—15 in high cards and 1 for the doubleton in Hearts. When your partner gives you a single raise, if you have a strong opening hand (16 to 18 points), rebid. Bid 3 Diamonds.

5 This hand contains 16 points in high cards. When your partner gives you a single raise, if you have a strong opening hand (16 to 18 points), rebid. Bid 2 No trump.

6 For an opening bid this hand contains 18 points—16 in high cards and 2 for the singleton in Hearts. After your partner has raised your suit, you can count 1 additional point for your fifth Spade. So your revalued hand contains 19 points. When your partner gives you a single raise, if your revalued hand is a very strong opening hand (19 to 21 points), jump. Bid 4 Spades.

WHAT IS YOUR REBID?

7 You opened 1 Spade.
Your partner responded 2 Spades.
Your opponents did not bid.

8 You opened 1 Spade.
Your partner responded 2 Spades.
Your opponents did not bid.

ANSWERS

7 For an opening bid this hand contains 18 points—16 in high cards and 2 for the singleton in Diamonds. After your partner has raised your suit, you can count 1 additional point for your fifth Spade. So your revalued hand contains 19 points. When your partner gives you a single raise, if your revalued hand is a very strong opening hand (19 to 21 points), jump. Bid 4 Spades.

8 This hand contains 19 points in high cards. When your partner gives you a single raise, if you have a very strong opening hand (19 to 21 points), jump. Bid 3 No trump.

Lesson 14

REBID BY OPENING BIDDER
AFTER ORIGINAL BID OF 1 IN A SUIT

When partner responds "one over one" or "two over one"

An opening bid of 1 in a suit may be made with hands ranging from 13 points to 22 points or more. Therefore, when you open with a bid of 1 in a suit you do not tell your partner how strong your hand is.

It is your first rebid that enables your partner to recognize the approximate strength of your hand. Your first rebid tells your partner to which class your hand belongs.

With a minimum hand (13 to 15 points)

Your rebid must be one which will allow your partner, if he too has a weak hand, to choose for the final contract 2 in his own suit or else 2 in the suit in which you made your opening bid.

Any of the following rebids will allow your partner to sign off at 1 of these 2 contracts. Therefore, if you make any of these rebids you tell him that you have a minimum hand.

Bid 1 in a new suit.

Bid 1 No trump.

Bid 2 in your own suit.

Bid 2 in your partner's suit.

Bid 2 in a new suit lower ranking than your original suit.

Do not bid 2 in a new suit higher ranking than your original suit, as this would prevent your partner from rebidding at the level of 2 in your first suit.

With a strong hand (16 to 18 points)

Your rebid must be one which will not allow your partner to rebid at the level of 2 in the suit in which you made your opening bid.

Do not bid 2 in a new suit lower ranking than your original suit, as this would allow your partner to bid 2 in your first suit.

Any of the following rebids will prevent your partner from rebidding 2 in your first suit. Therefore, if you make any of these rebids, you tell him that you have a strong hand.

Bid 2 in a new suit higher ranking than your original suit.

Bid 2 No trump, provided you can do so without jumping.

Some advanced players bid 2 No trump with only 15 points in high cards.

Bid 3 in your own suit.

Bid 3 in your partner's suit.

Bid 3 in a new suit, provided you can do so without jumping.

Some advanced players will not bid 3 in a new suit with less than 17 points.

With a very strong hand (19 to 21 points)

Your rebid should be a jump to 2 No trump if partner responded "one over one"; or 3 No trump if partner responded "two over one"; or a jump to 4 in your own major suit; or a jump to 4 in your partner's major suit; or a bid of 2 in a suit higher ranking than the suit you opened; or a bid in a new suit at the level of 3, provided you can do so without jumping.

If you make any of the following bids, you tell your partner that you have a very strong hand.

Jump to 2 No trump, if partner responded "one over one."

Jump to 3 No trump, if partner responded "two over one."

Jump to 4 in your partner's major suit.

Jump to 4 in your own major suit.

Bid 2 in a new suit higher ranking than your original suit.*

Bid 3 in a new suit without jumping.*

Do not jump in a new suit, unless you have a powerful hand (22 points or more).

With a powerful hand (22 points and up)

Your rebid should make it certain that game will be reached and should encourage your partner to explore the possibility of a slam; if he has a good hand.

* Note! These 2 rebids can be made with a strong hand (16 to 18 points) as well as with a very strong hand (19 to 21 points).

The following rebids tell your partner that you have a powerful hand.

Jump to 3 No trump, if partner responded "one over one."
Jump in a new suit.

A jump rebid in a new suit is forcing to game. It invites a slam.

Requirements for a jump

For a jump in your own suit you must have a strong six-card or a solid five-card suit.

For a jump in your partner's suit you must have four-card support for your partner's suit.

For a jump in No trump you must have strength in all unbid suits.

A jump rebid is not forcing to game, unless it is a jump in a new suit.

Rebid By Opening Bidder

AFTER ORIGINAL BID OF 1 IN A SUIT

When Partner Responds One Over One or Two Over One

13 to 15 points
  Bid 1 in a new higher ranking suit
  Bid 1 No trump
  Bid 2 in any suit, except a new higher ranking suit

16 to 18 points
  Bid 2 in a new higher ranking suit
  Bid 2 No trump, but don't jump
  Bid 3 in your own or in partner's suit
  Bid 3 in a new suit but don't jump

19 to 21 points
  Jump in No trump
  Jump to 4 in your own or in partner's major suit
  Bid 3 in a new suit, but don't jump
  Bid 2 in a new higher ranking suit

22 & up points
  Jump to 3 No trump after "one over one"
  Jump in a new suit

WHAT IS YOUR REBID?

A♠ Q♠ 10♠ 4♠ 5♥ 3♥ A♣ J♣ 9♣ 7♣ 6♣ 7♦ 3♦

1 You opened 1 Club.
Your partner responded 1 Heart.
Your opponents did not bid.

9♠ 8♠ A♥ K♥ 8♥ 6♥ K♣ J♣ 5♣ 4♣ K♦ 6♦ 3♦

2 You opened 1 Heart.
Your partner responded 1 Spade.
Your opponents did not bid.

8♠ 5♠ A♥ 10♥ 9♥ 5♥ 4♥ 8♣ 4♣ K♦ Q♦ J♦ 6♦

3 You opened 1 Heart.
Your partner responded 1 Spade.
Your opponents did not bid.

A♠ 7♠ 2♠ 7♥ A♣ K♣ 7♣ 5♣ 3♣ J♦ 6♦ 5♦ 3♦

4 You opened 1 Club.
Your partner responded 1 Spade.
Your opponents did not bid.

8♠ 5♠ A♥ K♥ 8♥ 5♥ 4♥ Q♣ 4♣ 2♣ Q♦ J♦ 6♦

5 You opened 1 Heart.
Your partner responded 2 Diamonds.
Your opponents did not bid.

ANSWERS

1 This hand contains 13 points—11 in high cards, 1 for the doubleton in Hearts, and 1 for the doubleton in Diamonds. With a minimum opening hand (13 to 15 points) your rebid must make it possible for your partner to choose for the final contract 2 in the suit you opened or 2 in his own suit. You can bid 1 in a new suit. Bid 1 Spade.

2 This hand contains 15 points—14 in high cards and 1 for the doubleton in Spades. With a minimum opening hand (13 to 15 points) your rebid must make it possible for your partner to choose for the final contract 2 in the suit you opened or 2 in his own suit. Your hand is suitable for No trump. Bid 1 No trump.

3 This hand contains 12 points—10 in high cards, 1 for the doubleton in Spades, and 1 for the doubleton in Clubs. With a minimum opening hand (13 to 15 points) your rebid must make it possible for your partner to choose for the final contract 2 in the suit you opened or 2 in his own suit. You can bid 2 in a new suit lower ranking than the suit you opened. Bid 2 Diamonds.

4 This hand contains 14 points—12 in high cards and 2 for the singleton in Hearts. With a minimum opening hand (13 to 15 points) your rebid must allow your partner, if he too has a weak hand, to choose for the final contract 2 in your original suit or (if this is impossible) 2 in his own suit. You have adequate support for your partner's Spade suit. Bid 2 Spades.

5 This hand contains 13 points—12 in high cards and 1 for the doubleton in Spades. With a minimum opening hand (13 to 15 points) your rebid must allow your partner, if he too has a weak hand, to choose for the final contract 2 in his own suit or (if this is impossible) 2 in the suit you opened. You can rebid your Hearts at the level of 2. Do not raise your partner to 3 Diamonds even though you have adequate trump support. Bid 2 Hearts.

WHAT IS YOUR REBID?

A♠ J♠ 9♠ 7♠ 6♠ 5♠ 4♠ 7♥ 3♣ A♦ Q♦ 10♦ 4♦

6 You opened 1 Spade.
Your partner responded 2 Hearts.
Your opponents did not bid.

K♠ 9♠ A♥ J♥ 9♥ 7♥ 5♥ A♣ 10♣ 6♣ 9♣ 8♦ 6♦

7 You opened 1 Heart.
Your partner responded 2 Diamonds.
Your opponents did not bid.

8♠ 6♠ A♥ Q♥ 8♥ 5♥ A♣ J♣ 9♣ 6♣ 5♣ A♦ 8♦

8 You opened 1 Club.
Your partner responded 1 Spade.
Your opponents did not bid.

A♠ 5♠ A♥ Q♥ J♥ 3♥ 2♥ J♣ 8♣ 5♣ K♦ Q♦ 7♦

9 You opened 1 Heart.
Your partner responded 2 Clubs.
Your opponents did not bid.

A♠ K♠ J♠ 4♠ 3♠ K♥ J♥ 3♥ 8♣ 2♣ K♦ J♦ 7♦

10 You opened 1 Spade.
Your partner responded 2 Hearts.
Your opponents did not bid.

ANSWERS

6 This hand contains 13 points—11 in high cards, 1 for the doubleton in Hearts, and 1 for the doubleton in Clubs. With a minimum opening hand (13 to 15 points) your rebid must make it possible for your partner to choose for the final contract 2 in the suit you opened or 2 in his own suit. You can rebid your Spades at the level of 2. With a minimum opening hand you must not bid 3 Diamonds. Bid 2 Spades.

7 This hand contains 13 points—12 in high cards and 1 for the doubleton in Spades. With a minimum opening hand (13 to 15 points) your rebid must make it possible for your partner to choose for the final contract 2 in the suit you opened or 2 in his own suit. You can rebid your Hearts. With a minimum opening hand you must not bid 2 No trump. Bid 2 Hearts.

8 This hand contains 17 points—15 in high cards, 1 for the doubleton in Spades, and 1 for the doubleton in Diamonds. With a strong opening hand (16 to 18 points) your rebid must make it impossible for your partner to rebid in the suit you opened at the level of 2. You can bid 2 in a suit higher ranking than the suit you opened. Bid 2 Hearts.

9 This hand contains 18 points—17 in high cards and 1 for the doubleton in Spades. With a strong opening hand (16 to 18 points) your rebid must make it impossible for your partner to rebid in the suit you opened at the level of 2. Your hand is suitable for No trump. Bid 2 No trump.

10 This hand contains 17 points—16 in high cards and 1 for the doubleton in Clubs. With a strong opening hand (16 to 18 points) your rebid must make it impossible for your partner to choose for the final contract 2 in the suit you opened. Therefore, do not bid 2 Spades. You have adequate trump support for your partner's Heart suit. Bid 3 Hearts.

WHAT IS YOUR REBID?

11 You opened 1 Heart.
Your partner responded 1 Spade.
Your opponents did not bid.

12 You opened 1 Club.
Your partner responded 1 Spade.
Your opponents did not bid.

13 You opened 1 Diamond.
Your partner responded 1 Spade.
Your opponents did not bid.

14 You opened 1 Diamond.
Your partner responded 2 Clubs.
Your opponents did not bid.

ANSWERS

11 This hand contains 17 points—15 in high cards, 1 for the doubleton in Spades, and 1 for the doubleton in Clubs. With a strong opening hand (16 to 18 points) your rebid must make it impossible for your partner to choose for the final contract 2 in the suit you opened. With a strong opening hand (16 to 19 points) and a strong 6-card trump suit, bid 3 in your own suit, even though a jump is required. Jump to 3 Hearts.

12 This hand contains 17 points—15 in high cards, 1 for the doubleton in Hearts, and 1 for the doubleton in Diamonds. With a strong opening hand (16 to 18 points) your rebid must make it impossible for your partner to choose for the final contract 2 in the suit you opened or 2 in his own suit. Therefore, do not bid 2 Clubs or 2 Spades. With a strong opening hand and more than adequate trump support for your partner's Spades, you can raise to 3 Spades, even though a jump is required. Bid 3 Spades.

13 This hand contains 20 points—19 in high cards and 1 for the doubleton in Spades. With a very strong opening hand (19 to 21 points), make a jump rebid. With a hand suitable for No trump, jump to 2 No trump over a "one over one" response.

14 This hand contains 20 points—19 in high cards and 1 for the doubleton in Clubs. With a very strong opening hand (19 to 21 points), make a jump rebid. With a hand suitable for No trump, jump to 3 No trump over a "two over one" response.

WHAT IS YOUR REBID?

| K♠ | Q♠ | 5♠ | 2♥ | 8♥ | 6♥ | A♣ | Q♣ | 6♣ | 4♣ | 2♣ | A♦ | Q♦ |

15 You opened 1 Club.
    Your partner responded 1 Spade.
    Your opponents did not bid.

| A♠ | Q♠ | J♠ | 5♠ | 4♠ | 3♠ | 2♥ | 9♣ | A♦ | K♦ | Q♦ | 5♦ | 2♦ |

16 You opened 1 Spade.
    Your partner responded 2 Hearts.
    Your opponents did not bid.

| Q♠ | 6♠ | A♥ | Q♥ | 10♥ | K♣ | Q♣ | 8♣ | 7♣ | A♦ | K♦ | J♦ | 2♦ |

17 You opened 1 Diamond.
    Your partner responded 1 Spade.
    Your opponents did not bid.

| A♠ | 4♠ | A♥ | K♥ | 10♥ | 8♥ | 5♥ | A♣ | K♣ | J♣ | 3♣ | 2♣ | 2♦ |

18 You opened 1 Heart.
    Your partner responded 1 Spade.
    Your opponents did not bid.

| 10♠ | A♥ | 10♥ | 9♥ | 8♥ | 6♥ | A♣ | K♣ | Q♣ | J♣ | J♦ | 7♦ | 3♦ |

19 You opened 1 Heart.
    Your partner responded 2 Diamonds.
    Your opponents did not bid.

ANSWERS

15 This hand contains 19 points—17 in high cards, 1 for the doubleton in Hearts, and 1 for the doubleton in Diamonds. With a very strong opening hand (19 to 21 points) and more than adequate trump support, you can jump to 4 in your partner's suit. Bid 4 Spades.

16 This hand contains 19 points—16 in high cards, 1 for the doubleton in Hearts, and 2 for the singleton in Clubs. With a very strong opening hand (19 to 21 points), you can bid 3 in a new suit, provided you do not have to jump to do so. Bid 3 Diamonds.

17 This hand contains 22 points—21 in high cards and 1 for the doubleton in Spades. With a powerful opening hand (22 points and up) and a hand suitable for No trump, jump to 3 No trump over a "one over one" response.

18 This hand contains 22 points—19 in high cards, 1 for the doubleton in Spades, and 2 for the singleton in Diamonds. With a powerful opening hand (22 points and up), you can jump in a new suit. Jump to 3 Clubs.

19 This hand contains 17 points—15 in high cards and 2 for the singleton in Spades. With a strong hand (16 to 18 points) you can bid 3 in a new suit, provided you can do so without jumping. Bid 3 Clubs.

Lesson 15

REBID BY RESPONDER
AFTER OPENING BID OF 1 IN A SUIT

With a minimum hand (6 to 9 points)

If your hand contains only 6 or 7 points, pass, unless your partner makes a forcing rebid (unless he makes a jump rebid in a new suit.)

If your hand contains 8 or 9 points, rebid, if your partner's own rebid invites you to do so (if your partner's rebid tells you that he holds better than a minimum hand).

With a strong hand (10 to 12 points)

If you have a stronge responding hand, rebid at least once.

With a very strong hand (13 to 15 points)

Because your partner made an opening bid, you can count on him for approximately 13 points. Since you too have 13 points, there are 26 points in the combined hands. Therefore, game is in sight.

On your first rebid, bid a new suit, or jump in a suit already bid.

Whenever the responder makes a bid in a new suit or jumps in a suit already bid, the opening bidder is forced to bid one more time.

With a powerful hand (16 to 18 points)

If your original response did not reveal the strength of your hand, make a big jump on your first rebid.

If your partner's rebid showed that he has a minimum hand, jump to game.

If your partner's rebid showed that he has a strong hand, explore the possibility of a slam.

With a tremendous hand (19 to 21 points)

Explore the possibility of a slam.

Requirements for a jump

For a jump in your own suit you must have a strong six-card or a solid five-card suit.

For a jump in your partner's suit you must have four-card support for your partner's suit.

For a jump in No trump you must have strength in all unbid suits.

Rebid by Responder

After Original Bid of 1 in a Suit by Partner

6 to 9 points..	Rebid if forced—with 6 or 7 points
	Rebid if invited—with 8 or 9 points
10 to 12 points..	Rebid at least once
13 to 15 points..	Jump in a suit already bid, or
	Rebid in new suits until game is reached
16 to 18 points..	Make big jump rebid
19 to 21 points..	Explore slam

WHAT IS YOUR REBID?

1 Your partner opened 1 Spade.
   You responded 2 Spades.
   Your partner bid 3 Spades.

ANSWER

1 This hand contains 6 points—5 in high cards and 1 for the doubleton in Hearts. With only 6 or 7 points do not rebid, unless your partner makes a jump rebid in a new suit, forcing you to rebid. Pass.

WHAT IS YOUR REBID?

10♠ 9♠ 8♠ 6♠ A♥ J♥ 4♥ 2♥ 10♣ 5♣ 4♣ 8♦ 7♦

2 Your partner opened 1 Diamond.
You responded 1 Heart.
Your partner bid 3 Clubs.

8♠ 3♠ 10♥ 8♥ 5♥ K♣ J♣ 5♣ 4♣ K♦ J♦ 7♦ 5♦

3 Your partner opened 1 Spade.
You responded 1 No trump.
Your partner bid 2 No trump.

8♠ 6♠ 10♥ 9♥ 8♥ 6♥ K♣ 5♣ 3♣ A♦ 9♦ 4♦ 2♦

4 Your partner opened 1 Heart.
You responded 2 Hearts.
Your partner bid 3 Clubs.

A♠ 7♠ 5♠ J♥ 5♥ 3♥ 10♣ 9♣ 7♣ 6♣ A♦ 10♦ 2♦

5 Your partner opened 1 Spade.
You responded 2 Spades.
Your partner bid 2 No trump.

A♠ 7♠ 5♠ Q♥ J♥ 3♥ 10♣ 9♣ 8♣ 6♣ Q♦ 10♦ 2♦

6 Your partner opened 1 Spade.
You responded 2 Spades.
Your partner bid 3 Spades.

ANSWERS

2 This hand contains 6 points—5 in high cards and 1 for the doubleton in Diamonds. Your partner's jump rebid in a new suit forces you to keep the bidding open until game is reached. Bid 3 No trump.

3 This hand contains 8 points in high cards. After you have responded 1 No trump, if your partner rebids, he invites you to bid again. With 8 or 9 points you can do so. Bid 3 No trump.

4 This hand contains 8 points—7 in high cards and 1 for the doubleton in Spades. After you have responded with a single raise, if your partner rebids, you know that he has a strong opening hand (16 to 18 points). He invites you to bid again. With 8 or 9 points you can do so. With 4-card support for his Heart suit, jump to game. Bid 4 Hearts.

5 This hand contains 9 points in high cards. After you have responded with a single raise, if your partner rebids, you know that he has a strong opening hand (16 to 18 points). He invites you to bid again. With 8 or 9 points you can do so. Bid 3 No trump.

6 This hand contains 9 points in high cards. After you have responded with a single raise, if your partner rebids, you know that he has a strong opening hand (16 to 18 points). He invites you to bid again. With 8 or 9 points you can do so. Your hand is suitable for No trump. Bid 3 No trump.

WHAT IS YOUR REBID?

A 8 6 5 8 3 9 8 7 K 8 7 6
♠ ♠ ♠ ♠ ♡ ♡ ♣ ♣ ♣ ♢ ♢ ♢

7 Your partner opened 1 Spade.
You responded 2 Spades.
Your partner bid 3 Spades.

J 5 4 A 9 5 4 2 K 5 4 7 6
♠ ♠ ♠ ♡ ♡ ♡ ♡ ♣ ♣ ♣ ♢ ♢

8 Your partner opened 1 Diamond.
You responded 1 Heart.
Your partner bid 2 Diamonds.

A K 10 6 3 7 6 4 8 6 Q 8 5
♠ ♠ ♠ ♠ ♠ ♡ ♡ ♡ ♣ ♣ ♢ ♢

9 Your partner opened 1 Heart.
You responded 1 Spade.
Your partner bid 2 Spades.

9 8 A 10 2 A 10 7 5 2 Q 6 3
♠ ♠ ♡ ♡ ♡ ♣ ♣ ♣ ♣ ♣ ♢ ♢

10 Your partner opened 1 Spade.
You responded 2 Clubs.
Your partner bid 3 Clubs.

K 10 8 6 9 8 A Q 10 2 J 6 5
♠ ♠ ♠ ♠ ♡ ♡ ♣ ♣ ♣ ♣ ♢ ♢

11 Your partner opened 1 Heart.
You responded 1 Spade.
Your partner bid 2 Spades.

ANSWERS

7 This hand contains 8 points—7 in high cards and 1 for the doubleton in Hearts. After you have responded with a single raise, if your partner rebids, you know that he has a strong opening hand (16 to 18 points). He invites you to bid again. With 8 or 9 points you can do so. Bid 4 Spades.

8 This hand contains 9 points—8 in high cards and 1 for the doubleton in Diamonds. When your partner rebids in his own suit at the level of 2, you know that he has a minimum opening hand (13 to 15 points). He does not invite you to bid again. Pass.

9 This hand contains 10 points—9 in high cards and 1 for the doubleton in Clubs. When your partner on his first rebid raises your own suit to the level of 2, you know that he has a minimum opening hand (13 to 15 points). Nevertheless, when you have a strong responding hand (10 to 12 points), you should rebid at least once. Bid 3 Spades.

10 This hand contains 11 points—10 in high cards and 1 for the doubleton in Spades. When your partner on his first rebid makes it impossible for you to rebid 2 in his suit or 2 in your own suit, you know that he has a strong opening hand (16 to 18 points). In the combined hands you know that you have at least 26 points. Your hand is suitable for No trump. Bid 3 No trump.

11 This hand contains 11 points—10 in high cards and 1 for the doubleton in Hearts. When your partner on his first rebid raises your suit to the level of 2, you know that he has a minimum opening hand (13 to 15 points). Nevertheless, when you have a strong responding hand (10 to 12 points) you should rebid at least once. Bid 3 Clubs.

WHAT IS YOUR REBID?

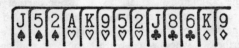

12 Your partner opened 1 Diamond.
You responded 1 Heart.
Your partner bid 2 Diamonds.

13 Your partner opened 1 Club.
You responded 1 Heart.
Your partner bid 1 No trump.

14 Your partner opened 1 Heart.
You responded 1 Spade.
Your partner bid 2 Spades.

15 Your partner opened 1 Club.
You responded 1 Diamond.
Your partner bid 1 No trump.

16 Your partner opened 1 Spade.
You responded 2 Hearts.
Your partner bid 2 Spades.

ANSWERS

12 This hand contains 12 points—11 in high cards and 1 for the doubleton in Diamonds. When your partner rebids at the level of 2 in his own suit, you know that he has a minimum opening hand (13 to 15 points). Nevertheless, when you have a strong responding hand (10 to 12 points) you should rebid at least once. Bid 2 No trump.

13 This hand contains 12 points—11 in high cards and 1 for the doubleton in Clubs. When your partner bids 1 No trump, you know that he has a minimum opening hand (13 to 15 points). Nevertheless, when you have a strong responding hand (10 to 12 points), you should rebid at least once. Bid 2 No trump.

14 This hand contains 13 points—12 in high cards and 1 for the doubleton in Clubs. When your partner on his first rebid raises your suit to the level of 2, you know that he has a minimum opening hand (13 to 15 points). Nevertheless, since you have 26 points in the combined hands, jump to game in your suit. Bid 4 Spades.

15 This hand contains 14 points—13 in high cards and 1 for the doubleton in Spades. When your partner bids 1 No trump, you know that he has a minimum opening hand (13 to 15 points). Nevertheless, you have 26 points in the combined hands. Your hand is suitable for No trump. Jump to 3 No trump.

16 This hand contains 13 points—12 in high cards and 1 for the doubleton in Diamonds. When your partner bids 2 in his own suit, you know that he has a minimum opening hand (13 to 15 points). Nevertheless, you have 26 points in the combined hands. Your partner has a rebiddable Spade suit, so jump to game in this suit. You can make this jump with only 3 trumps, because your partner rebid his suit before you raised it. Bid 4 Spades.

WHAT IS YOUR REBID?

17 Your partner opened 1 Spade.
You responded 2 Clubs.
Your partner bid 2 Diamonds.

ANSWERS

17 This hand contains 17 points—14 in high cards and 3
for the singleton in Hearts. When your partner's rebid
makes it possible for you to bid 2 in his original suit,
you know that he has a minimum opening hand (13 to
15 points). Nevertheless, you have a powerful responding hand (16 to 18 points). So make a big jump rebid.
Bid 4 Spades. This is not a sign-off.

Lesson 16

REBID BY RESPONDER
WHEN PARTNER HAS BID 2 SUITS

Show preference

The suit eventually chosen for trumps should, if possible, be the one in which you and your partner together, in your combined hands, hold the greatest number of trumps.

Therefore, whenever your partner has bid 2 suits, and the hand is to be played with one of his suits as trumps, you should always let him know in which of these 2 suits you think the combined hands hold the most trumps.

If you have unequal length in the 2 suits your partner bid, show a preference for the suit in which you, yourself, have the greatest number of cards.

If you have equal length in the 2 suits your partner bid, show a preference for your partner's original suit, since that is probably his longest suit.

When your hand is so weak that you want to sign off

If you prefer the suit your partner bid last, sign off by passing.

If you prefer the suit your partner bid first, sign off by making the lowest possible bid in partner's original suit. This is considered the same as a pass.

When your hand is strong enough for a real raise

If you want to show your partner a positive raise as well as a preference, you must raise the level of the bidding as well as raising the suit itself.

If you prefer the suit your partner bid last, give him a single raise in that suit. This will automatically raise the level of the bidding.

If you prefer the suit your partner bid first, give him a jump raise in his original suit. A jump raise will be necessary to raise the level of the bidding. A jump raise in this case is considered the same as a single raise, because in this case a single raise merely shows a preference and is considered the same as a pass.

Rebid by Responder

After Partner Has Bid 2 Suits - Show Preference

With unequal length—prefer your own longer suit
With equal length—prefer your partner's first suit

WHAT IS YOUR REBID?

Q♠ J♠ 8♠ 6♠ A♥ 8♥ 7♥ 5♣ 3♣ 2♣ 7♦ 6♦ 5♦

1 Your partner opened 1 Heart.
You responded 1 Spade.
Your partner bid 2 Diamonds.

10♠ 9♠ 8♠ 6♠ 7♥ 6♥ 5♥ A♣ Q♣ 3♣ 2♣ 9♦ 8♦

2 Your partner opened 1 Heart.
You responded 1 No trump.
Your partner bid 2 Diamonds.

10♠ 9♠ 8♠ K♥ J♥ 3♥ 8♣ 4♣ 3♣ A♦ 8♦ 3♦ 2♦

3 Your partner opened 1 Spade.
You responded 1 No trump.
Your partner bid 2 Hearts.

ANSWERS

1   This hand contains 8 points—7 in high cards and 1 for
    the doubleton in Hearts. When your partner's rebid
    allows you to rebid in his first suit at the level of 2, you
    know that he has a minimum opening hand (13 to 15
    points). He does not invite you to bid again. With 8 or
    9 points you should sign off. You prefer your partner's
    Diamonds to his Hearts, because you hold more Dia-
    monds. Therefore, pass.

2   This hand contains 7 points—6 in high cards and 1 for
    the doubleton in Diamonds. When your partner's rebid
    allows you to rebid in his first suit at the level of 2, you
    know that he has a minimum opening hand (13 to 15
    points). He does not invite you to bid again. With 7
    points you should sign off. You prefer your partner's
    Hearts to his Diamonds, because you hold more Hearts.
    Sign off by bidding 2 Hearts. This shows a preference,
    not a true raise.

3   This hand contains 8 points in high cards. When your
    partner's rebid allows you to rebid in his first suit at the
    level of 2, you know that he has a minimum opening
    hand (13 to 15 points). He does not invite you to bid
    again. With 8 or 9 points you should sign off. With
    equal length in your partner's Spades and Hearts you
    prefer his Spades, because that is the suit he bid first.
    Sign off by bidding 2 Spades. This shows a preference,
    not a true raise.

WHAT IS YOUR REBID?

4 Your partner opened 1 Heart.
You responded 1 Spade.
Your partner bid 2 Diamonds.

5 Your partner opened 1 Heart.
You responded 1 Spade.
Your partner bid 2 Diamonds.

6 Your partner opened 1 Heart.
You responded 2 Diamonds.
Your partner bid 3 Clubs.

ANSWERS

4 This hand contains 11 points in high cards. When your partner's rebid allows you to return to his first suit at the level of 2, you know that he has a minimum opening hand (13 to 15 points). He does not invite you to bid again. Nevertheless, with a strong responding hand (10 to 12 points), you should rebid at least once. With equal length in your partner's Hearts and Diamonds, you prefer his Hearts, because that is the suit he bid first. To show a true raise instead of a mere preference, you must raise the level of the bidding. Therefore, bid 3 Hearts.

5 This hand contains 10 points—9 in high cards and 1 for the doubleton in Clubs. When your partner's rebid allows you to return to his first suit at the level of 2, you know that he has a minimum opening hand (13 to 15 points). He does not invite you to bid again. Nevertheless, with a strong responding hand (10 to 12 points) you should rebid at least once. You prefer your partner's Diamonds to his Hearts, because you hold more Diamonds. Raise in the normal way. Bid 3 Diamonds.

6 This hand contains 10 points—9 in high cards and 1 for the doubleton in Clubs. When your partner rebids at the level of 3 in a new suit, you know that he has a strong opening hand (16 to 18 points). With a strong responding hand (10 to 12 points) you should rebid at least once. You prefer your partner's Hearts to his Clubs, because you hold more Hearts. To show a true raise instead of a mere preference, you must raise the level of bidding. Therefore, bid 4 Hearts.

Lesson 17

OPENING BID OF 2 IN A SUIT

When you think that you can probably make a game, even without support from your partner, and think you could probably make a slam if your partner can help, open by bidding 2 in a suit.

An opening bid of 2 in a suit is the strongest bid you can make. It forces both you and your partner to keep the bidding open at least until game is reached.

An opening bid of 2 in a suit requires a very high point count. Moreover, it should seldom be made without a long, strong trump suit.

With a strong five-card trump suit—25 points are required.

With a strong six-card trump suit—23 points are required.

With a strong seven-card trump suit—21 points are required.

One less point is required if you have another good five-card suit in addition to the trump suit.

For an opening bid of 2 in a minor suit, the requirements are two points higher than the above.

Opening Bid of 2 in a Suit

25 points—With a strong 5-card suit
23 points—With a strong 6-card suit
21 points—With a strong 7-card suit

WHAT IS YOUR OPENING BID?

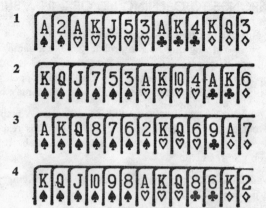

ANSWERS

1   This hand contains 25 points—24 in high cards and 1 for the doubleton in Spades. It contains a strong 5-card suit. Open 2 Hearts.

2   This hand contains 23 points—20 in high cards, 1 for for the doubleton in Clubs, and 2 for the singleton in Diamonds. It contains a strong six-card suit. Open 2 Spades.

3   This hand contains 21 points—18 in high cards, 2 for the singleton in Clubs, and 1 for the doubleton in Diamonds. It contains a strong seven-card suit. Open 2 Spades.

4   This hand contains 20 points—18 in high cards, 1 for the doubleton in Clubs, and 1 for the doubleton in Diamonds. Do not open 2 Spades. Open 1 Spade.

Lesson 18

RESPONSE TO OPENING BID OF 2 IN A SUIT

If your partner has made an opening bid of 2 in a suit, his hand is so strong that he can probably make a game, even without any help from you.

Therefore, you are forced to keep the bidding open until game is reached, no matter how weak your hand may be.

If you have a worthless hand, bid 2 No trump. A response of 2 No trump is a discouraging negative bid. This response warns your partner not to try for a slam, because he cannot count on you for help.

If you have 8 points, you may make an encouraging positive response.
With adequate trump support, raise partner to 3.
With a biddable suit, bid your own suit.
With neither trump support nor a biddable suit, jump to 3 No trump.

Response to Opening of 2 in a Suit

Less than 8 points	Bid 2 No trump
8 points—With no biddable suit..	Bid 3 No trump
8 points—With a biddable suit...	Bid your suit
8 points—With trump support...	Bid 3 in partner's suit

WHAT IS YOUR RESPONSE?

1 Your partner opened 2 Spades.
Next player passed.

8♠ 7♠ 3♠ 9♡ 6♡ 3♡ 2♡ 8♣ 4♣ 3♣ 6♢ 5♢ 3♢

2 Your partner opened 2 Spades.
Next player passed.

9♠ 8♠ 6♠ 10♡ 9♡ 7♡ 4♡ Q♣ 5♣ 3♣ A♢ Q♢ 5♢

ANSWERS

1 This hand contains no points. Nevertheless, you must not pass. When your partner opens by bidding 2 in a suit you must keep the bidding open until game is reached. With less than 8 points respond 2 No trump.

2 This hand contains 8 points in high cards. It does not contain a biddable suit. With 8 points but no biddable suit, respond 3 No trump.

WHAT IS YOUR RESPONSE?

3   Your partner opened 2 Hearts.
    Next player passed.

4   Your partner opened 2 Spades.
    Next player passed.

ANSWERS

3   This hand contains 8 points—7 in high cards and 1 for
    the doubleton in Diamonds. Your Spade suit is biddable.
    With 8 points and a biddable suit, respond in your suit.
    Respond 2 Spades.

4   This hand contains 8 points—7 in high cards and 1 for
    the doubleton in Hearts. You have adequate trump sup-
    port for your partner. With 8 points and trump support,
    raise your partner's suit. Respond 3 Spades.

Lesson 19

OPENING BID OF 2 NO TRUMP

An opening bid of 2 No trump does not force your partner to respond. It does, however, show great strength.

An opening bid of 2 No trump is made only when you have precisely the following requirements:

You must have not less than 22 and not more than 24 points in high cards only.

You must have No trump distribution (5-3-3-2) or (4-4-3-2) or (4-3-3-3).

You must have every suit stopped.

When you have 25 to 27 high card points, No trump distribution, and a sure stopper in all 4 suits, open 3 No trump, unless you have a strong five-card suit.

When you have 25 to 27 points and a strong five-card suit, you can open with a bid of 2 in a suit.

Opening Bid of 2 No Trump

22 to 24 points in high cards only—No more & no less
Balanced hand—(5-3-3-2) or (4-4-3-2) or (4-3-3-3)
All suits stopped

WHAT IS YOUR OPENING BID?

1 A♠ Q♠ A♡ K♡ 9♡ 6♡ K♣ 10♣ 8♣ K♦ Q♦ J♦ 9♦

2 A♠ Q♠ 8♠ 2♠ A♡ Q♡ J♡ K♣ Q♣ 7♣ A♦ Q♦ 6♦

3 A♠ 6♠ A♡ K♡ Q♡ 5♡ J♣ 10♣ 2♣ A♦ K♦ Q♦ 4♦

4 A♠ Q♠ A♡ K♡ 10♡ 9♡ A♣ 5♣ 3♣ K♦ J♦ 5♦ 4♦

ANSWERS

1 This hand contains 22 points in high cards. It has No trump distribution and stoppers in all suits. Open 2 No trump.

2 This hand contains 24 points in high cards. It has No trump distribution and stoppers in all suits. Open 2 No trump.

3 This hand contains 23 points in high cards. It has No trump distribution. Do not open 2 No trump, because the Club suit is not stopped. Open 1 Heart.

4 This hand contains 21 points in high cards. It has No trump distribution and stoppers in all suits. Do not open 2 No trump, because you do not have 22 to 24 points in high cards. Open 1 Heart.

Lesson 20

RESPONSE TO OPENING BID OF 2 NO TRUMP

If your partner has made an opening bid of 2 No trump, you may pass only if you hold a worthless hand.

If your hand will help your partner in any way at all, you must respond, because in this case he will surely make a game. Whenever you hold 4 points you should respond.

If you have less than 4 points—Pass, or bid a six-card major suit. A six-card major can be bid, even though you do not have any points at all.

If you have 4 points or more—Bid 3 No trump, or bid a five-card major suit.

If you have 10 points—Explore the possibility of a slam. Bid 4 No trump.

If you have 11 or 12 points—Bid 6 No trump, or Bid 6 in a long strong suit.

Response to opening bid of 3 No Trump

If you have less than 6 points—Pass.
If you have 6 or 7 points—Bid 4 No trump.
If you have 8 or 9 points—Bid 6 No trump, or
                                   Bid 6 in a long strong suit.

After an opening bid in No trump, a 4 No trump bid is not the Blackwood Convention asking your partner to tell you how many aces he holds. A bid of 4 No trump invites your partner to jump directly to a slam.

Response to Opening Bid of 2 No Trump

Less than 4 points............	Pass, or Bid 6-card major
4 points or more........	Bid 3 No trump, or Bid 3 in 5-card major
10 points	Bid 4 No trump
11 or 12 points	Bid 6 No trump, or Bid 6 in long strong suit

WHAT IS YOUR RESPONSE?

Your Partner Opened 2 No Trump. Next Player Passed.

1 — J♠ 10♠ 6♠ 6♥ 5♥ 2♥ 9♣ 8♣ 4♣ Q♦ 8♦ 4♦ 3♦

2 — Q♠ 9♠ 6♠ 5♠ 2♠ Q♥ 3♥ 8♣ 6♣ 5♣ 5♦ 4♦ 2♦

3 — 10♠ 9♥ 8♥ 7♥ 6♥ 5♥ 2♥ 8♣ 5♣ 4♣ 10♦ 5♦ 3♦

4 — 7♠ Q♥ 6♥ 5♥ 3♥ 2♥ 8♣ 5♣ 4♣ Q♦ 10♦ 8♦ 7♦

5 — Q♠ J♠ 6♠ 5♠ 2♠ 10♥ 9♥ 9♣ 7♣ 5♣ 8♦ 6♦ 4♦

6 — 10♠ 2♠ 9♥ 8♥ 6♥ 3♥ K♣ J♣ 7♣ 5♣ 3♣ 9♦ 7♦

7 — A♠ 8♠ 4♠ K♥ 9♥ 7♥ 4♥ Q♣ 8♣ 6♣ 5♦ 3♦ 2♦

8 — K♠ J♠ 7♠ 4♠ 5♥ 4♥ A♣ K♣ 10♣ 7♣ 8♦ 7♦ 3♦

ANSWERS

1   This hand contains 3 points in high cards. With less than 4 points and a balanced hand, pass.

2   This hand contains 4 points in high cards. With 4 points and a balanced hand, respond 3 No trump.

3   This hand contains no points in high cards. However, with a 6-card major suit, respond 3 Hearts.

4   This hand contains 4 points in high cards. With 4 points and an unbalanced hand containing a 5-card major suit, bid your suit. Respond 3 Hearts.

5   This hand contains 3 points in high cards. With less than 4 points in high cards and a balanced hand, pass.

6   This hand contains 4 points in high cards. It is an unbalanced hand. With 4 points but no 5-card major suit, respond 3 No trump. Do not respond in a minor suit.

7   This hand contains 9 points in high cards. With 10 points, or even 9 points, you can bid 4 No trump.

8   This hand contains 11 points in high cards. With 11 or 12 points, bid 6 No trump.

Lesson 21

PREEMPTIVE OPENING BID OF 3 IN A SUIT

Opening bids of 3 in a suit are preemptive bids which are made to shut out the opponents and keep them from bidding.

Preemptive bids are made with the full realization that it may be impossible to make the contract.

Such bids are made with hands that are weak except for one long suit. But the hand must still be strong enough so that the contract cannot be set more than 2 tricks if you are vulnerable, or 3 tricks if you are not vulnerable, even if your partner can take no tricks at all.

Do not make a preemptive bid if you have the requirements for an opening bid of 1 in a suit, or if you have 10 points in high cards (without counting points for short suits or voids).

For a preemptive opening bid of 3 in a suit you must have a long suit and approximately 10 points in high cards and short suits combined. You must hold at least 6 trumps if you are not vulnerable, or 7 trumps if you are vulnerable.

For a 3 bid in a minor suit you must hold at least 2 of the 3 top honors in that suit. But these honors are not required for an opening bid of 3 in a major suit.

Preemptive bids are sometimes made by opening with 4 in a suit, if 8 or 9 trumps are held. An opening bid of 4 in a minor suit does not require 2 of the three top honors.

Opening Bid of 3 in a Suit

Without the requirements for an opening bid of 1 in a suit
With less than 10 points in high cards

10 points approximately
  6 trumps if not vulnerable; 7 trumps if vulnerable
  2 of the 3 top honors, if a minor suit is bid

WHAT IS YOUR OPENING BID?

1 Q♠ J♠ 10♠ 8♠ 7♠ 3♠ 8♥ A♣ 7♣ J♦ 10♦ 7♦ 4♦

2 Q♠ J♠ 10♠ 8♠ 7♠ 3♠ 8♥ A♣ 7♣ K♦ 10♦ 7♦ 4♦

3 A♠ 10♠ 9♠ 6♥ 5♥ 7♥ 2♣ K♦ Q♦ 10♦ 9♦ 4♦ 2♦

ANSWERS

1 This hand contains 11 points—8 in high cards, 2 for the singleton in Hearts, and 1 for the doubleton in Clubs. You cannot make an opening bid of 1 Spade. You have less than 10 points in high cards. You have approximately 10 points in all. You have a strong 6-card major suit. Open 3 Spades.

2 This hand contains 13 points—10 in high cards, 2 for the singleton in Hearts, and 1 for the doubleton in Clubs. Do not open 3 Spades, because you can make an opening bid of 1 in a suit. Open 1 Spade.

3 This hand contains 11 points—9 in high cards, 1 for the doubleton in Hearts, and 1 for the doubleton in Clubs. You cannot make an opening bid of 1 Diamond. You have less than 10 points in high cards. You have approximately 10 points in all. You have a strong 6-card Diamond suit with 2 of the 3 top honors. Open 3 Diamonds.

WHAT IS YOUR OPENING BID?

4 ♠8 ♥J ♥10 ♥7 ♥4 ♣A ♣7 ♦Q ♦J ♦10 ♦8 ♦7 ♦3

5 ♥7 ♥5 ♥2 ♣7 ♣5 ♣3 ♦A ♦K ♦J ♦7 ♦6 ♦5 ♦4

6 ♠J ♠4 ♠2 ♥7 ♥5 ♥9 ♣7 ♣A ♦K ♦Q ♦J ♦5 ♦3

ANSWERS

4 This hand contains 11 points—8 in high cards, 2 for the singleton in Spades, and 1 for the doubleton in Clubs. You cannot make an opening bid of 1 Diamond. You have less than 10 points in high cards. You have approximately 10 points in all. You have a strong 6-card Diamond suit. But do not open 3 Diamonds, because you do not have 2 of the 3 top honors. Pass.

5 This hand contains 11 points—8 in high cards and 3 for the void in Spades. You cannot make an opening bid of 1 Diamond. You have less than 10 points in high cards. You have approximately 10 points in all. You have a strong 7-card Diamond suit in which you hold 2 of the 3 top honors. Open 3 Diamonds.

6 This hand contains 13 points—11 in high cards, 1 for the doubleton in Clubs, and 1 for the doubleton in Hearts. Do not make an opening bid of 3 Diamonds because you have 11 points in high cards and can make an opening bid of 1 in a suit. Open 1 Diamond.

Lesson 22

RESPONSE TO PREEMPTIVE OPENING BID
OF 3 IN A SUIT

Since a preemptive opening bid by your partner of 3 in a suit indicates weakness and not strength, usually you should pass.

However, game may still be within reach, if you have a very strong responding hand (13 to 15 points).

After an opening bid of 3 in a minor

If you have a very strong responding hand 16 to 18 points) and a strong rebiddable major suit, bid 3 in your major suit.

If you have a very strong responding hand (13 to 15 points) including Ax, Kx, or Qx in partner's suit, bid 3 No trump.

Do not raise your partner's minor suit.

After an opening bid of 3 in a major

If you have a very strong responding hand (13 to 15 points) raise your partner's major suit. This raise can be given even though you do not have any trump support for your partner.

When your partner opens with a preemptive bid, do not try for a slam, unless you have a powerful responding hand (16 to 18 points) including 3 Aces, or 2 Aces and the K or Q in your partner's suit.

Response to Opening Bid of 3 in a Suit

When Partner Opens with 3 in Minor
16 to 18 points—With a strong rebiddable major
    Bid 3 in major
13 to 15 points—With Ax, Kx, or Qx, in partner's suit
    Bid 3 No trumps
When Partner Opens With 3 in Major
13 to 15 points—Raise to 4 . . . . Even without trump support

WHAT IS YOUR RESPONSE?

A K Q 5 2 ♠ | 8 6 2 ♥ | J 4 ♣ | 10 9 8 ♦

1 Your partner opened 3 Clubs.
Next player passed.

K 5 2 ♠ | A K Q 7 5 ♥ | 7 4 3 ♣ | 9 7 ♦

2 Your partner opened 3 Diamonds.
Next player passed.

A 9 7 2 ♠ | Q 9 8 5 ♥ | Q 6 ♣ | K Q 4 ♦

3 Your partner opened 3 Clubs.
Next player passed.

A Q J 7 2 ♠ | 8 ♥ | K 7 3 ♣ | K 8 7 5 ♦

4 Your partner opened 3 Hearts.
Next player passed.

A Q 6 5 2 ♠ | 6 4 ♥ | 8 6 4 ♣ | K J 6 ♦

5 Your partner opened 3 Hearts.
Next player passed.

J 10 8 7 6 2 ♠ | 3 ♥ | K 2 ♣ | A 10 6 4 ♦

6 Your partner opened 3 Clubs.
Next player passed.

ANSWERS

1 This hand contains 11 points—10 in high cards and 1 for the doubleton in Clubs. Even though you have a strong rebiddable Spade suit, do not respond 3 Spades, because you do not have a very strong responding hand (13 to 15 points). Do not bid 3 No trump, because you do not have a very strong responding hand (13 to 15 points) nor do you have 1 of the 3 top honors in your partner's minor suit. Pass.

2 This hand contains 13 points—12 in high cards and 1 for the doubleton in Diamonds. It is a very strong responding hand (13 to 15 points) and contains a strong rebiddable major suit. Nevertheless, pass.

3 This hand contains 13 points in high cards. You have Q6 in your partner's Club suit. With a very strong responding hand (13 to 15 points) and one of the 3 top honors in partner's minor suit accompanied by a low card, respond 3 No trump.

4 This hand contains 13 points in high cards. You cannot count any points for the singleton in your partner's suit, if you expect his suit to be the trump suit. Do not bid your Spades. You know your partner's suit is longer than your own. With a very strong responding hand (13 to 14 points), raise your partner to 4 in his major suit, even though you do not have trump support. Respond 4 Hearts.

5 This hand contains 10 points in high cards. You cannot count any points for the doubleton in your partner's suit, if you expect his suit to be the trump suit. Do not respond, unless you have a very strong responding hand (13 to 15 points), even though you have a good Spade suit. Pass.

6 This hand contains 11 points—8 in high cards, 2 for the singleton in Hearts, and 1 for the doubleton in Clubs. Do not bid 3 Spades or 3 No trump. You do not have a very strong responding hand (13 to 15 points). Pass.

Lesson 23

MINIMUM OVERCALL

If your opponents have opened the bidding, the chances are that they hold more points than you and your partner.

Nevertheless, you want to show your partner your best suit if possible, so he will know which suit to lead to you. Also you want to interfere with your opponents' bidding.

Therefore, if you can do so with reasonable safety, make a minimum overcall. A minimum overcall is a suit bid higher than the opponent's bid, but not a jump bid.

In deciding whether to overcall, you should consider the strength of your trump suit as more important than the number of points you hold.

Never overcall in a four-card suit.

Even when you are not vulnerable and overcall at the level of 1, you should hold a rebiddable trump suit.

When you are vulnerable or when you overcall at the level of 2, you should hold a really strong rebiddable suit. You should not expect to lose more than 2 trump tricks when trumps are led.

You can make a minimum overcall with only 10 to 12 points, which is less than the number of points required for an opening bid. Minimum overcalls are usually made with comparatively weak hands. Occasionally, however, they are made with hands strong enough for an opening bid.

Minimum Overcall

10 to 12 points—with rebiddable suit

WHAT IS YOUR BID?

1 Your right hand opponent opened 1 Diamond. You are not vulnerable.

2 Your right hand opponent opened 1 Club. You are not vulnerable.

3 Your right hand opponent opened 1 Heart. You are vulnerable.

ANSWERS

1 This hand contains 11 points—10 in high cards and 1 for the doubleton in Clubs. Do not overcall. Your Spade suit is not strong enough. Pass.

2 This hand contains 10 points—9 in high cards, and 1 for the doubleton in Clubs. You have a rebiddable Spade suit. If your partner should get the opening lead you want him to lead Spades. Overcall 1 Spade.

3 This hand contains 11 points—8 in high cards, 1 for the doubleton in Hearts, and 2 for the singleton in Clubs. If your partner should get the opening lead you want him to lead Spades. Your Spade suit is strong enough for an overcall, even though you are vulnerable. Overcall 1 Spade.

WHAT IS YOUR BID?

4   Your right hand opponent opened 1 Heart.
You are not vulnerable.

5   Your right hand opponent opened 1 Diamond.
You are not vulnerable.

6   Your right hand opponent opened 1 Spade.
You are vulnerable.

ANSWERS

4   This hand contains 13 points—11 in high cards, 1 for the doubleton in Hearts, and 1 for the doubleton in Diamonds. If your partner should get the opening lead, you want him to lead Clubs. Your Club suit is strong enough for an overcall at the level of 2. Overcall 2 Clubs.

5   This hand contains 14 points—13 in high cards and 1 for the doubleton in Hearts. Do not overcall in a 4-card suit. Pass.

6   This hand contains 14 points—12 in high cards, and 2 for the singleton in Spades. Your Heart suit is not strong enough for an overcall when you are vulnerable. Pass.

Lesson 24

RESPONSE TO MINIMUM OVERCALL

When your partner has made a minimum overcall, which is a weak bid, he may not have many points in high cards; but on the other hand, he has a good trump suit. The responses to minimum overcalls are based on this assumption.

Therefore, in order to respond to a minimum overcall you should have a better hand than is required for a response to an opening bid.

For a response in No trump

You must have a strong responding hand (10 to 12 points). You must also have a sure stopper in any suit bid by your opponents.

A response of 1 No trump, when your opponents have bid, shows strength not weakness.

For a raise in your partner's suit

You must have a strong responding hand (10 to 12 points).

However, a raise may be given with 1 trump less than adequate support, because you know that your partner has at least 5 trumps.

For a bid in your own suit

You must always have a rebiddable suit.

If your suit is higher ranking than your partner's and can be shown without raising the level of the bidding, you must have a strong responding hand (10 to 12 points).

If your suit is lower ranking than your partner's and must be shown at a higher level of bidding, you must have a very strong responding hand (13 to 15 points).

If you can raise your partner, do not bid a suit of your own unless your partner has bid a minor suit and you have a strong rebiddable major suit.

Response to Minimum Overcall

No Trump Take-out

10 to 12 points.. With sure stopper in opponent's suit

Single Raise in Partner's Suit

10 to 12 points.. With 1 trump less than adequate support

Suit Take-out

10 to 12 points.. With a strong rebiddable suit—at same level
13 to 15 points.. With a strong rebiddable suit—at higher level

---

WHAT IS YOUR BID?

Q 7 3 ♠ 8 2 ♥ J 10 8 4 ♣ A 8 7 5 ♦

1 Your 1st opponent opened 1 Heart.
Your partner overcalled 1 Spade.
Your 2nd opponent passed.

A Q 10 ♠ A 9 7 ♥ 10 8 5 4 2 ♣ 8 7 ♦

2 Your 1st opponent opened 1 Spade.
Your partner overcalled 2 Diamonds.
Your 2nd opponent passed.

K Q 7 5 3 ♠ 7 5 2 ♥ A ♣ 10 J 4 3 ♦

3 Your 1st opponent opened 1 Club.
Your partner overcalled 1 Heart.
Your 2nd opponent passed.

7♠ 4♠ A♡ Q♡ 10♡ 8♡ 5♡ K♣ 8♣ 7♣ 3♣ 7♢ 2♢

4 Your 1st opponent opened 1 Spade.
Your partner overcalled 2 Diamonds.
Your 2nd opponent passed.

ANSWERS

1 This hand contains 8 points—7 in high cards and 1 for
the doubleton in Hearts. Do not raise your partner's
Spades, because you do not have a strong responding
hand (10 to 12 points). Pass.

2 This hand contains 11 points—10 in high cards, and 1
for the doubleton in Diamonds. You have a sure stopper
in your opponent's suit. With a strong responding hand
(10 to 12 points) in high cards and a stopper in your
opponent's suit, respond 2 No trump.

3 This hand contains 11 points—10 in high cards, and 1
for the doubleton in Clubs. Do not respond 1 Spade. If
you can raise your partner's major suit, do not bid a
suit of your own. An overcall can be raised with 1
trump less than the trumps required to raise an opening
bid. With a strong responding hand (10 to 12 points)
and adequate trump support for an overcall, raise your
partner to 2 Hearts.

4 This hand contains 11 points—9 in high cards, 1 for
the doubleton in Spades, and 1 for the doubleton in Diamonds. You have a rebiddable suit which is higher
ranking than your partner's so it can be shown without
raising the level of the bidding. Therefore, with a strong
responding hand (10 to 12 points) you can bid your own
suit. Bid 2 Hearts.

WHAT IS YOUR BID?

K♠ 6♠ 3♠ 9♡ 7♡ 5♡ A♣ K♣ Q♣ 4♣ 2♣ 8♦ 2♦

5 Your 1st opponent opened 1 Heart.
Your partner overcalled 2 Diamonds.
Your 2nd opponent passed.

K♠ 6♠ 3♠ 8♡ 3♡ 2♡ A♣ K♣ Q♣ 4♣ 2♣ 8♦ 2♦

6 Your 1st opponent opened 1 Diamond.
Your partner overcalled 1 Heart.
Your 2nd opponent passed.

A♠ K♠ J♠ 10♠ 2♠ 10♡ 9♡ 8♡ 7♡ 5♣ J♣ 9♦ 2♦

7 Your 1st opponent opened 1 Club.
Your partner overcalled 1 Diamond.
Your 2nd opponent passed.

A♠ K♠ J♠ 10♠ 2♠ 10♡ 9♡ 8♡ 7♡ 5♣ J♣ 9♦ 2♦

8 Your 1st opponent opened 1 Club.
Your partner overcalled 1 Heart.
Your 2nd opponent passed.

K♠ 6♠ 3♠ 8♡ 3♡ 2♡ A♣ K♣ J♣ 4♣ 2♣ 8♦ 3♦

9 Your 1st opponent opened 1 Heart.
Your partner overcalled 2 Diamonds.
Your 2nd opponent passed.

ANSWERS

5 This hand contains 13 points—12 in high cards and 1 for the doubleton in Diamonds. You cannot support your partner's Diamonds. You have a strong rebiddable Club suit. With a very strong responding hand (13 to 15 points) and a strong, rebiddable suit, you can bid your own suit, even though you raise the level of the bidding. Bid 3 Clubs.

6 This hand contains 13 points—12 in high cards and 1 for the doubleton in Diamonds. You have a very strong responding hand (13 to 15 points). However, do not bid your Club suit. If you can raise your partner's major suit, do not bid a suit of your own. An overcall can be raised with 1 trump less than the trumps required to raise an opening bid. Raise your partner to 2 Hearts.

7 This hand contains 10 points—9 in high cards, and 1 for the doubleton in Clubs. Since an overcall can be raised with 1 trump less than the trumps required to raise an opening bid, you have adequate trump support to raise your partner's Diamonds. However, with a strong rebiddable major suit of your own, it is better to bid your major suit. With a strong responding hand (10 to 12 points) bid 1 Spade.

8 This hand contains 10 points—9 in high cards and 1 for the doubleton in Clubs. Do not bid Spades. If you can raise your partner, do not bid a suit of your own, unless your partner bid a minor suit and you have a strong rebiddable major. An overcall can be raised with 1 trump less than the trumps required to raise an opening bid. With a strong responding hand (10 to 12 points) and adequate trump support for an overcall, raise your partner to 2 Hearts.

9 This hand contains 12 points—11 in high cards and 1 for the doubleton in Diamonds. Do not bid Clubs. It requires a very strong responding hand (13 to 15 points) to bid a suit lower ranking than your partner's, because to do so you must raise the level of the bidding. Therefore, pass.

Lesson 25

STRONG OVERCALLS

Take-out double

A take-out double is an informatory double which forces your partner to take the double out and keep the bidding open.

A double is recognized as a take-out double and not a business double if all 3 of the following conditions apply:
You doubled at your first opportunity to double that suit.
You doubled before your partner made a bid or doubled.
You doubled a suit bid of not more than 3.

When your opponents have opened the bidding, and you hold 13 to 15 points or more, make a take-out double, provided your hand also meets one or the other of the two following requirements:

1—a **minimum hand** (13 to 15 points) which will make a good dummy for any suit your partner can bid, because it has adequate trump support for all suits except the suit bid by your opponent.

2—a **strong hand** (16 to 18 points) which contains a strong rebiddable suit in which you can safely play the hand, if you don't like your partner's response to your take-out double.

No trump overcall

When your opponents have opened the bidding and you hold a hand which meets all the requirements for an opening bid of 1 No trump (16 to 18 points, balanced distribution, and 3 suits stopped), overcall with a bid of 1 No trump, provided you have a sure stopper in your opponent's suit.

Jump overcall

A jump overcall (after one of your opponents has opened the bidding) is a jump bid in a suit—that is, a bid 1 trick higher than is necessary to keep the bidding open.

For years a jump overcall was used to show a very strong hand with one or sometimes two strong rebiddable suits. Now (when you overcall) a takeout double is the only way to show such a hand.

A jump overcall (like an opening preemptive bid) is now made with a hand that is weak except for one long, strong suit. But the hand must still be strong enough so that the contract can not be set more than 2 tricks if you are vulnerable, or 3 tricks if you are not vulnerable, even if your partner can take no tricks at all.

For a jump overcall you must have a long suit and approximately 10 points in high cards and short suits combined. You must hold at least 6 trumps if you are not vulnerable, or 7 trumps if you are vulnerable.

Do not make a jump overcall if you have the requirements for an opening bid of 1 in a suit, or if you have 10 points in high cards alone (without counting points for short suits or voids).

If you know that your partner is not an up-to-date player, do not make a jump overcall, even though you have the necessary requirements. Make a minimum overcall instead.

Strong Overcall

Take-out Double

13 to 15 points	With support for all 3 suits not bid by opponent, or
16 to 18 points	With a strong rebiddable suit

Jump Overall

Approx. 10 points	With 7 trumps if vulnerable
	With 6 trumps if not vulnerable

No Trump Overcall

16 to 18 points	With requirements for opening bid of 1 No trump
	With sure stopper in opponent's suit

WHAT IS YOUR BID?

Q♠ J♠ 4♠ 3♠ 7♥ A♣ K♣ 8♣ 6♣ J♦ 9♦ 7♦ 4♦

1 Your right hand opponent opened 1 Heart.

A♠ K♠ Q♠ 8♠ 7♠ Q♥ J♥ 3♥ 9♣ 8♣ 7♣ 10♦ 8♦

2 Your right hand opponent opened 1 Diamond.

A♠ K♠ 10♠ 9♠ 7♠ 5♠ 9♥ Q♣ 7♣ 3♣ A♦ Q♦ 7♦

3 Your right hand opponent opened 1 Heart.

A♠ Q♠ 9♠ 8♠ 7♠ A♥ J♥ 8♥ 5♥ 4♥ Q♣ 9♣ 3♣

4 Your right hand opponent opened 1 Diamond.

A♠ J♠ J♥ 9♥ 6♥ 4♥ K♣ Q♣ J♣ 5♣ A♦ J♦ 6♦

5 Your right hand opponent opened 1 Diamond.

A♠ 9♠ 7♠ 4♠ 3♠ A♥ K♣ 6♣ 4♣ J♦ 10♦ 8♦ 3♦

6 Your right hand opponent opened 1 Spade.

ANSWERS

1 This hand contains 13 points—11 in high cards and 2 for the singleton in Hearts. With a minimum opening hand (13 to 15 points) and adequate trump support for all suits except the one bid by your opponent, make a take-out double. Double.

2 This hand contains 13 points—12 in high cards and 1 for the doubleton in Diamonds. Do not bid 1 Spade, because you have the requirements for a take-out double. Double.

3 This hand contains 17 points—15 in high cards and 2 for the singleton in Hearts. It contains a strong rebiddable Spade suit. It meets the requirements for a take-out double. Double.

4 This hand contains 16 points—13 in high cards and 3 for the void in Diamonds. You have adequate trump support for all suits except the suit bid by your opponent. Make a take-out double.

5 This hand contains 17 points in high cards. It meets all the requirements for an opening bid of 1 No trump. It contains a sure stopper in the suit your opponent bid. Overcall 1 No trump.

6 This hand contains 14 points—12 in high cards and 2 for the singleton in Hearts. Do not make a take-out double. You do not have adequate trump support for Hearts, nor do you have a strong rebiddable suit. Do not overcall in Clubs or Diamonds, because they are four-card suits. Pass.

WHAT IS YOUR BID?

K 10 9 8 2 Q 5 J 6 5 A Q 2
♠ ♠ ♠ ♠ ♠ ♡ ♡ ♣ ♣ ♣ ♢ ♢ ♢

7 Your right hand opponent opened 1 Diamond.

7 5 2 7 5 3 A K J 7 6 5 4
♡ ♡ ♡ ♣ ♣ ♣ ♢ ♢ ♢ ♢ ♢ ♢ ♢

8 Your right hand opponent opened 1 Spade.

ANSWERS

7 This hand contains 13 points—12 in high cards and 1 for the doubleton in Hearts. Do not make a take-out double, because you do not have adequate trump support for Hearts and Clubs, nor do you have a strong rebiddable suit. Do not overcall 1 Spade; your Spade suit is not strong enough. Pass.

8 This hand contains 11 points—8 in high cards and 3 for the void in Spades. Your hand is weak except for a long, strong Diamond suit. You do not have the requirements for an opening bid of 1 Diamond. You have less than 10 points in high cards alone. You have approximately 10 points in all. You have a strong seven-card suit. Make a jump overcall in Diamonds. Bid 3 Diamonds.

However, if you know that your partner is not an up-to-date player, do not make a jump overcall. Make a minimum overcall. Bid 2 Diamonds.

Lesson 26

RESPONSE TO STRONG OVERCALLS

Response to overcall of 1 No trump

The requirements for a response to an overcall of 1 No trump are exactly the same as the requirements for a response to an opening bid of 1 No trump.

Response to jump overcall

The requirements for a response to a jump overcall are the same as the requirements for a response to an opening preemptive bid of 3 in a major suit. Pass, unless you have a very strong responding hand (13 to 15 points). With 13 to 15 points or more, raise your partner's suit. This raise can be given without trump support for your partner's suit.

However, if you know that your partner (not up-to-date) still uses a jump overcall as a strong bid and not as a preemptive bid, respond practically the same as you would to an opening bid of 1 in a suit.

When you respond to a jump overcall by a partner who is not up-to-date:

A minimum responding hand (6 to 9 points) is required for a response in No trump, a single raise, or a response in a higher ranking suit at the same level.

A strong responding hand (10 to 12 points) is required for a response in a lower ranking suit at a higher level.

There are, however, the following differences between an old-fashioned response to a jump overcall and a response to an opening bid:

1—For a response in No trump you must have a stopper in your opponents' suits.
2—Since your partner surely has a long suit, 1 less trump is required to raise your partner's suit.
3—Don't respond in a new suit, unless you cannot raise your partner's suit and you have a strong rebiddable suit of your own.

Response to take-out double

When your opponent has opened the bidding and your partner has made a take-out double, there are only two conditions under which you may pass:

1—When you have great length and strength in your opponent's suit, and expect to set the contract.
2—When the opponent on your right redoubles or bids, and you have a worthless hand.

Otherwise, you must take-out the the double by bidding your longest and strongest suit, or by bidding No trump. But do not bid No trump, unless you have a strong responding hand (10 to 12 points) and a stopper in your opponent's suit.

Advanced players sometimes respond 1 No trump with 8 or 9 points.

If you have a strong responding hand (10 to 12 points) and a biddable suit, show your partner this strength by making a jump bid in your suit.

Response to Strong Overcall

When Partner Overcalls With 1 No Trump
Same as response to opening bid of 1 No trump

When Partner Makes Jump Overcall
13 to 15 points.. Even without trump support—Raise partner

When Partner Makes Take-out Double
Great length and strength in opponent's suit.........Pass
 0 to 9 points ....Bid longest suit
10 to 12 points..With stopper in opponent's suit ... Bid No trump
10 to 12 points..With a biddable suit .... Jump in a suit

WHAT IS YOUR BID?

A♠ 6♠ J♥ 8♥ 7♥ 6♥ 3♥ K♣ 10♣ 8♣ 5♣ 8♦ 2♦

1   Your 1st opponent opened 1 Club.
    Your partner overcalled 1 No trump.
    Your 2nd opponent passed.

J♠ 10♠ 8♠ 7♠ 9♥ 6♥ 4♥ A♣ 3♣ Q♦ 10♦ 8♦ 2♦

2   Your 1st opponent opened 1 Heart.
    Your partner overcalled 1 No trump.
    Your 2nd opponent passed.

ANSWERS

1   This is an unbalanced hand. It contains 9 points—8 in
    high cards and 1 for the five-card Heart suit. A response
    to an overcall of 1 No trump is the same as a response
    to an opening bid of 1 No trump. With 8 or 9 points
    respond 2 No trump.

2   This is a balanced hand. It contains 7 points in high
    cards. A response to an overcall of 1 No trump is the
    same as a response to an opening bid of 1 No trump.
    With a balanced hand and less than 8 points, pass.

WHAT IS YOUR BID?

7 2 ♠ A 6 ♥ 4 7 5 ♣ 4 K 10 6 5 3 ♦

3 Your 1st opponent opened 1 Heart.
Your partner overcalled 2 Spades.
Your 2nd opponent passed.

A 8 4 3 ♠ 7 6 4 3 ♥ Q ♣ 8 5 3 2 ♦

4 Your 1st opponent opened 1 Club.
Your partner overcalled 2 Hearts.
Your 2nd opponent passed.

A Q 8 7 6 2 ♠ 5 3 ♥ 10 8 5 ♣ 3 6 ♦

5 Your 1st opponent opened 1 Diamond.
Your partner overcalled 2 Hearts.
Your 2nd opponent passed.

9 8 7 ♠ 9 8 3 2 ♥ 9 7 4 ♣ 8 7 3 ♦

6 Your 1st opponent opened 1 Club.
Your partner doubled.
Your 2nd opponent passed.

A 6 ♠ Q J 10 3 2 ♥ 7 5 4 ♣ 10 8 7 ♦

7 Your 1st opponent opened 1 Heart.
Your partner doubled.
Your 2nd opponent passed.

ANSWERS

3 This hand contains 7 points in high cards. Do not count any points for the doubleton in Spades, because that is your partner's suit. Do not respond to a jump overcall unless you have a very strong responding hand (13 to 15 points). Pass.

However, if you know that your partner (not up-to-date) still uses a jump overcall as a strong bid and not a preemptive bid, respond 2 No trump.

4 This hand contains 8 points—6 in high cards and 2 for the singleton in Clubs. Do not respond to a jump overcall, unless you have a very strong responding hand (13 to 15 points). Pass.

However, if you know that your partner (not up-to-date) still uses a jump overcall as a strong bid and not a preemptive bid, raise your partner to 3 Hearts.

5 This hand contains 9 points—6 in high cards, 1 for the doubleton in Hearts, and 2 for the singleton in Diamonds. Do not respond to a jump overcall, unless you have a very strong responding hand (13 to 15 points). Pass.

However, if you know that your partner (not up-to-date) still uses a jump overcall as a strong bid and not a preemptive bid, respond 2 Spades.

6 This hand contains no points at all. Nevertheless, you must not pass. Respond in your longest suit. Bid 1 Heart.

7 This hand contains 8 points—7 in high cards and 1 for the doubleton in Spades. You have great length and strength in your opponent's Heart suit and expect to set the contract. Pass.

WHAT IS YOUR BID?

8 Your 1st opponent opened 1 Club.
Your partner doubled.
Your 2nd opponent passed.

9 Your 1st opponent opened 1 Diamond.
Your partner doubled.
Your 2nd opponent passed.

ANSWERS

8 This hand contains 10 points in high cards. You have a strong responding hand (10 to 12 points) in high cards. You have a stopper in your opponent's Club suit. You do not have a biddable suit. Bid 1 No trump.

9 This hand contains 10 points in high cards. You have a biddable Spade suit. With a strong responding hand (10 to 12 points) and a biddable suit, make a jump bid in your suit, even though it is only a four-card suit. Bid 2 Spades.

Lesson 27

FREE RESPONSES

A free bid is a bid you make which is not necessary in order to keep the bidding open—that is, when your partner will have another chance to bid even though you should pass.

The opportunity to make a free response occurs whenever the opponent on your right overcalls your partner's opening bid, or makes a take-out double of your partner's opening bid, or injects a bid or redouble following a take-out double by your partner.

WHEN YOUR PARTNER HAS OPENED THE BIDDING

If your right hand opponent overcalls

For a free response you should have a strong responding hand (10 to 12 points). For a free bid of 1 No trump you must also have a stopper in the suit bid by your opponent.

Advanced players make a free response at the level of 1 in a suit, or a free raise from 1 to 2 in partner's suit, with as little as 9 points.

If your right hand opponent makes a take-out double

With 10 to 12 points redouble instead of bidding.

Redouble even though you do not hold adequate trump support for your partner.

With less than 10 points ignore the take-out double and respond as you would have responded if the take-out double had not been made.

WHEN YOUR PARTNER HAS MADE A TAKE-OUT DOUBLE

If your right hand opponent bids or redoubles

With 6 to 9 points respond if your right hand opponent bids.

With even less, respond if your right hand opponent redoubles, provided only one of your suits is suitable for trumps.

Free Bids

When Partner Opens and Opponent Overcalls
10 to 12 points....... Make free response

When Partner Opens and Opponent Makes Take-out Double
10 to 12 points....... Redouble
Otherwise............ Ignore take-out double

When Partner Makes Take-out Double and Opponent Bids or Redoubles
 6 to 9 points....... Respond if opponent bids
Even less............ Respond if opponent redoubles

WHAT IS YOUR BID?

♠ 10 ♠ 8 ♠ 6 ♠ 5 ♥ 7 ♥ 9 ♣ 8 ♣ 6 ♣ 3 ♣ K ◇ J ◇ 4 ◇ 3

1 Your partner opened 1 Spade.
Your right hand opponent overcalled 2 Clubs.

♠ 10 ♠ 8 ♠ 6 ♠ 5 ♥ 8 ♥ 6 ♣ K ♣ J ♣ 2 ◇ A ◇ 5 ◇ 3 ◇ 2

2 Your partner opened 1 Spade.
Your right hand opponent overcalled 2 Clubs.

♠ A ♠ 10 ♠ 7 ♠ 6 ♠ 5 ♥ J ♥ 5 ♥ 3 ♣ Q ♣ J ♣ 5 ◇ 8 ◇ 6

3 Your partner opened 1 Diamond.
Your right hand opponent overcalled 1 Heart.

♠ Q ♠ J ♠ 2 ♥ 8 ♥ 6 ♥ 4 ♥ A ♣ 9 ♣ 5 ♣ 4 ◇ K ◇ 5 ◇ 2

4 Your partner opened 1 Heart.
Your right hand opponent overcalled 1 Spade.

ANSWERS

1 This hand contains 7 points—4 in high cards and 3 for the singleton in Hearts. A free raise requires more points than the minimum required to raise an opening bid. Pass.

2 This hand contains 9 points—8 in high cards and 1 for the doubleton in Hearts. A free raise requires more points than the minimum required to raise an opening bid. Pass.

However, advanced players raise from 1 to 2 in partner's suit with as little as 9 points.

3 This hand contains 9 points—8 in high cards and 1 for the doubleton in Diamonds. A free response at the level of 1 requires more points than a "one over one" response to an opening bid. Pass.

However, advanced players would bid 1 Spade with 9 Points.

4 This hand contains 10 points in high cards. A free response of 1 No trump after your opponent has overcalled shows strength, not weakness. It should not be made with less than 10 points. It shows a strong responding hand (10 to 12 points) and a stopper in your opponent's suit. Respond 1 No trump.

WHAT IS YOUR BID?

8 5 3 ♠ **8 2** ♥ **Q 5 2** ♣ **A K J 6 5** ♦

5 Your partner opened 1 Heart.
Your right hand opponent overcalled 1 Spade.

7 6 ♠ **A K 6 5 3** ♥ **Q 6 5 4** ♣ **10 9** ♦

6 Your partner opened I Diamond.
Your right hand opponent overcalled 1 Spade.

8 5 3 ♠ **8 2** ♥ **K 5 2** ♣ **A K J 6 5** ♦

7 Your partner opened 1 Spade.
Your right hand opponent overcalled 2 Hearts.

8 5 3 ♠ **8 2** ♥ **7 4 2** ♣ **A K J 6 5** ♦

8 Your partner opened 1 Heart.
Your right hand opponent overcalled 1 Spade.

K 9 8 3 ♠ **5** ♥ **A 7 6 2** ♣ **K 7 6 3** ♦

9 Your partner opened 1 Heart.
Your right hand opponent doubled.

A 10 8 6 5 ♠ **8 3** ♥ **K 5 2** ♣ **Q J 2** ♦

10 Your partner opened 1 Heart.
Your right hand opponent doubled.

ANSWERS

5 This hand contains 11 points—10 in high cards and 1 for the doubleton in Hearts. A free response in a new suit at the level of 2 requires a strong responding hand (10 to 12 points). Respond 2 Diamonds.

6 This hand contains 11 points—9 in high cards, 1 for the doubleton in Spades, and 1 for the doubleton in Diamonds. A free response in a new suit at the level of 2 requires a strong responding hand (10 to 12 points). Respond 2 Hearts..

7 This hand contains 12 points—11 in high cards, and 1 for the doubleton in Hearts. A free response at the level of 3 requires 12 points. Respond 3 Diamonds.

8 This hand contains 9 points—8 in high cards and 1 for the doubleton in Hearts. A free bid in a new suit at the level of 2 requires a strong responding hand (10 to 12 points). Pass.

9 This hand contains 10 points in high cards. Do not count any points for the singleton in Hearts, because that is your partner's suit. If your right hand opponent doubles your partner's opening bid, whenever you hold a strong responding hand (10 to 12 points), redouble.

10 This hand contains 11 points—10 in high cards and 1 for the doubleton in Hearts. Do not respond 1 Spade. If your right hand opponent doubles your partner's opening bid, whenever you hold a strong responding hand (10 to 12 points), redouble.

WHAT IS YOUR BID?

8♠ 7♠ 9♡ 8♡ 5♡ Q♣ 8♣ 7♣ 6♣ Q♦ J♦ 3♦ 2♦

11 Your partner opened 1 Spade.
    Your right hand opponent doubled.

8♠ 3♠ 10♡ 8♡ 7♡ 6♡ Q♣ 9♣ 8♣ K♦ J♦ 5♦ 2♦

12 Your partner opened 1 Heart.
    Your right hand opponent doubled.

A♠ 10♠ 7♠ 5♠ 3♠ 9♡ 2♡ Q♣ J♣ 3♣ 8♦ 6♦ 2♦

13 Your partner opened 1 Heart.
    Your right hand opponent doubled.

A♠ 10♠ 7♠ 5♠ 3♠ 4♡ 3♡ 5♣ 3♣ 2♣ 5♦ 3♦ 2♦

14 Your 1st opponent opened 1 Club.
    Your partner doubled.
    Your 2nd opponent bid 1 Heart.

A♠ 10♠ 7♠ 5♠ 5♡ 4♡ K♣ 6♣ 3♣ 7♦ 5♦ 4♦ 2♦

15 Your 1st opponent opened 1 Heart.
    Your partner doubled.
    Your 2nd opponent bid 2 Hearts.

A♠ 10♠ 7♠ 5♠ 10♡ 8♡ 7♡ 5♡ 8♣ 6♣ 6♦ 3♦ 2♦

16 Your 1st opponent opened 1 Heart.
    Your partner doubled.
    Your 2nd opponent bid 2 Hearts.

ANSWERS

11 This hand contains 5 points in high cards. Do not count any points for the doubleton in Spades, because that is your partner's suit. With a minimum responding hand (6 to 9 points), ignore your opponent's take-out double. Respond as you normally would to an opening bid. Pass.

12 This hand contains 7 points—6 in high cards and 1 for the doubleton in Spades. With a minimum responding hand (6 to 9 points), ignore your opponent's take-out double. Respond as you normally would to an opening bid. Raise your partner to 2 Hearts.

13 This hand contains 8 points—7 in high cards and 1 for the doubleton in Hearts. With a minimum responding hand (6 to 9 points), ignore your opponent's take-out double. Respond as you normally would to an opening bid. Respond 1 Spade.

14 This hand contains 5 points—4 in high cards and 1 for the doubleton in Hearts. When your partner has made a take-out double, and then your right hand opponent bids, if you have less than a minimum responding hand (6 to 9 points), pass.

15 This hand contains 8 points—7 in high cards and 1 for the doubleton in Hearts. When your partner has made a take-out double, and then your right hand opponent bids following the take-out double, if you have a minimum responding hand (6 to 9 points), you should respond to the take-out double. Bid 2 Spades.

16 This hand contains 5 points—4 in high cards and 1 for the doubleton in Clubs. When your partner has made a take-out double, and then your right hand opponent bids following the take-out double, if you have less than a minimum responding hand (6 to 9 points), pass.

WHAT IS YOUR BID?

J5 3 8 5 3 2 J 10 7 Q 9 4
♠ ♠ ♥ ♥ ♥ ♥ ♥ ♣ ♣ ♣ ♦ ♥ ♦

17 Your 1st opponent opened 1 Heart.
Your partner doubled.
Your 2nd opponent redoubled.

Q 10 9 5 3 8 7 6 J 7 6 5 3
♠ ♠ ♠ ♠ ♠ ♠ ♥ ♥ ♥ ♣ ♣ ♣ ♦ ♦

18 Your 1st opponent opened 1 Club.
Your partner doubled.
Your 2nd opponent redoubled.

ANSWERS

17 This hand contains 4 points in high cards. When your
partner has made a take-out double, and then your right
hand opponent has redoubled, if you have less than a
minimum responding hand (6 to 9 points) you should
pass, unless you want to recommend positively one of
your suits for trumps. If you have a strong desire to
name the trump suit, bid your suit, even though you
have less than 6 points. With this hand, pass.

18 This hand contains 4 points—3 in high cards and 1 for
the doubleton in Diamonds. When your partner has
made a take-out double, and then your right hand opponent has redoubled, if you have less than a minimum
responding hand (6 to 9 points), you should pass, unless you want to recommend positively one of your
suits for trumps. In this case bid your suit, even though
you have less than 6 points. Respond 1 Spade.

Lesson 28

PENALTY DOUBLE

A penalty double should be made only when you are confident that you can set your opponents at least 2 tricks.

To determine whether this can be done, you rely not only on your own hand, but also on the number of tricks which your partner's bids indicate that he can take.

If your partner has made an opening bid, count on him for 3 tricks if he opened with a suit bid, or 4 tricks if he opened with 1 No trump.

If your partner made a take-out double, count on him for 3 tricks.

If your partner responded to an opening bid of your own, count on him for 1 trick if he has shown a minimum responding hand, or 2 tricks if he has shown a strong responding hand.

If your partner overcalled an opponent's opening bid, count on him for 1 trick.

When the contract is in a suit, count your partner's tricks, plus your own tricks outside the trump suit, plus the number of trump tricks you expect to take.

When the contract is in No trump, count your partner's tricks plus your own high-card tricks. Add 2 low-card tricks, if you have a strong suit in the combined hands.

However, one situation frequently arises when you should double, even though you are not confident that you can set your opponents 2 tricks.

Sometimes your partner opens the bidding, and your right hand opponent overcalls with the same bid which you would have made as a response to your partner's opening bid.

In this case double without hesitation, unless the doubled contract, if it is not defeated, will give your opponents a game.

Double for Penalty

When you can set opponents 2 tricks, or
When your partner opens and your opponent's overcall is the same
as the response you expected to make

WHAT IS YOUR BID?

1 You are South.

The previous bidding has been as follows:

EAST	SOUTH	WEST	NORTH
1 Club	1 Diamond	2 Clubs	2 Diamonds
2 No trump	Pass	3 No trump	Pass
Pass	?		

2 You are South

The previous bidding has been as follows:

NORTH	EAST	SOUTH	WEST
1 Heart	1 Spade	Pass	2 Clubs
2 Diamonds	2 Spades	Pass	3 Spades
Pass	4 Spades	?	

9♣ 5♠ 4♠ 3♠ A♥ 9♥ 8♥ A♥ 4♣ 3♣ Q♣ 4♦ 2♦

3 You are South.

The previous bidding has been as follows:

NORTH	EAST	SOUTH	WEST
1 Club	1 Spade	2 Clubs	2 Diamonds
Pass	2 No trump	Pass	3 No trump
Pass	Pass	?	

ANSWERS

1 This hand contains 11 points—9 in high cards, 1 for the doubleton in Hearts, and 1 for the doubleton in Spades. Because your partner raised your overcall, you know that he can support your Diamond suit, and you can probably count on him to take 2 tricks. Your own hand will probably take 4 Diamond tricks and 1 Club trick. Therefore, your partnership will probably take 7 tricks —more than enough to set your opponents by 2 tricks. Therefore, double.

2 This hand contains 6 points—5 in high cards, and 1 for the doubleton in Diamonds. Because your partner made an opening bid, you can probably count on him to take 3 tricks. Your own hand will probably take at least 2 tricks, possibly 3 tricks—2 tricks in Spades and 1 trick with the K of Diamonds. Therefore, your partnership will probably take at least 5 tricks—enough to set your opponents by 2 tricks. Therefore, double.

3 This hand contains 10 points in high cards. Because your partner made an opening bid, you can probably count on him to take 3 tricks. Your own hand will take 2 sure tricks, but probably no more. Therefore, your partnership will probably take 5 tricks. But this will set your opponents only 1 trick, so do not double. Pass.

WHAT IS YOUR BID?

A♠ 2♠ K♥ 10♥ 6♥ 4♥ 9♣ 7♣ 5♣ A♦ Q♦ 8♦ 4♦

4 You are South.

The previous bidding has been as follows:

EAST	SOUTH	WEST	NORTH
1 Heart	Pass	3 Hearts	Pass
4 Hearts	?		

8♠ 5♠ A♥ 9♥ 7♥ 5♥ 3♥ J♣ 10♣ 7♣ 6♣ 4♣ 9♦

5 Your partner opened 1 Diamond.
Your right hand opponent overcalled 1 Heart.

ANSWERS

4 This hand contains 14 points—13 in high cards and 1 for the doubleton in Spades. You cannot count on your partner for any tricks, because he did not bid. You can probably count on taking 4 tricks in your own hand— 2 trump tricks, 1 Spade trick, and I Diamond trick. This is not enough to set your opponents 2 tricks, so do not double. Pass.

5 This hand contains 8 points—5 in high cards, 1 for the doubleton in Spades, and 2 for the singleton in Diamonds. If your right hand opponent had not overcalled, you would have responded 1 Heart. Therefore, double without hesitation.

Lesson 29

SLAM BIDDING AT TRUMP CONTRACT

Before you can safely bid a slam, you must determine by the preliminary bidding that in the combined hands you have the following requirements:

For a small slam, 33 points. For a grand slam, 37 points.

For a small slam, first-round control in 3 suits and second-round control in the 4th.

For a grand slam, first-round control in all 4 suits.

If the hand is to be played at a trump contract, the combined hands must also have:

A long, strong trump suit in which the opponents will probably not take a trick.

A strong side suit, which can be quickly established without losing more than 1 trick.

The number of points in the combined hands, the trump strength, and the strong side suit should be recognized by the time the bidding reaches the level of 4.

The first and second-round control is then explored by the Blackwood Convention.

Under the Blackwood system, when either player bids 4 No trump, his partner makes a response which tells the number of Aces he holds. Then, likewise, when the player who has bid 4 No trump follows with a bid of 5 No trump, his partner makes a response which tells the number of Kings he holds.

After a bid of 4 no trump

> With 0 Aces—respond 5 Clubs.
> With 1 Ace —respond 5 Diamonds.
> With 2 Aces—respond 5 Hearts.
> With 3 Aces—respond 5 Spades.
> With 4 Aces—respond 5 Clubs.

After a bid of 5 no trump

> With 0 Kings—respond 6 Clubs.
> With 1 King —respond 6 Diamonds.
> With 2 Kings—respond 6 Hearts.
> With 3 Kings—respond 6 Spades.
> With 4 Kings—respond 6 Clubs.

The possibility of a slam can often be recognized by certain bids.

If you are the opening bidder, you should be alert for the possibility of a slam, if your partner:
Jumps in a new suit.
Makes a bid in a suit already bid by an opponent.
Makes a jump response in No trump or in your suit, unless you hold a minimum hand (13 to 15 points).

If *you are the responding bidder,* you should be alert for a slam if your partner:
Opens with 2 in a suit or 2 No trump.
Makes a jump rebid in a new suit.
Makes a jump rebid in a suit already bid or in No trump, provided your hand is as good as an opening bid (13 to 15 points).

Slam Bidding

Small Slam

33 points
A very strong trump suit
A strong side suit
1st-round control in 3 suits
2nd-round control in 4th suit

Grand Slam

37 points
A very strong trump suit
A strong side suit
1st-round control in all 4 suits

WHAT IS YOUR BID?

1 You are South.

The previous bidding has been as follows:

NORTH	EAST	SOUTH	WEST
1 Spade	Pass	2 Diamonds	Pass
3 Spades	Pass	?	

ANSWERS

1 This hand contains 15 points—12 in high cards and 3 for the singleton in Hearts. Your partner's jump rebid indicates that he has a strong opening hand (16 to 18 points) and a strong six-card or solid five-card Spade suit. With your support for his Spades, his hand, if revalued, will contain 1 or perhaps 3 additional points. In the combined hands you have a long, strong Spade suit for trumps. You have a strong side suit in Diamonds. If your partner has 18 points, you have 33 points in the combined hands. Therefore, explore the possibility of a slam. Bid 4 No trump.

WHAT IS YOUR BID?

2 You are South.

The previous bidding has been as follows:

SOUTH	WEST	NORTH	EAST
1 Heart	Pass	3 Hearts	Pass

3 You are South.

The previous bidding has been as follows:

SOUTH	WEST	NORTH	EAST
1 Club	Pass	2 Spades	Pass
?			

4 You are South.

The previous bidding has been as follows:

SOUTH	WEST	NORTH	EAST
1 Heart	Pass	2 No trump	Pass
?			

ANSWERS

2 For an opening bid this hand contains 14 points—12 in high cards and 2 for the singleton in Spades. After your partner has raised your Hearts, you can count 1 additional point for your fifth Heart, and 2 additional points for your sixth Heart, making the revalued hand contain 17 points. Your partner's jump response in your suit shows that he has a very strong responding hand (13 to 15 points), but no more. You cannot count on 33 points in the combined hands. You have a powerful trump suit, but you probably do not have a strong side suit. Do not try for slam. Bid 4 Hearts.

3 This hand contains 14 points—13 in high cards and 1 for the doubleton in Hearts. Your partner's jump response in a new suit shows you that he has a tremendous responding hand (19 to 21 points) and a long, strong trump suit for which you have a good support. You can count at least 33 points in the hand, and you have a strong side suit in Clubs. Explore the possibility of a slam. Bid 4 No trump.

4 This hand contains 20 points in high cards. Your partner's jump response of 2 No trump shows you that he has a very strong responding hand (13 to 15 points) in high cards. You can count at least 33 points in the combined hands, so explore the possibility of a slam in No trump. Bid 4 No trump.

Quiz 1

♥ 9 ♥ 7 ♥ 6 ♠ A ♠ K ♠ J ♠ 8 ♦ A ♦ 8 ♦ 6 ♣ 6 ♣ 3 ♣ 2

1 **WHAT IS YOUR REBID?**
   Your partner opened 1 Club.
   You responded 1 Spade.
   Your partner bid 1 No trump.

2 **WHAT IS YOUR OPENING BID?**

3 **WHAT IS YOUR RESPONSE?**
   Your partner opened 1 Heart.

4 **WHAT IS YOUR RESPONSE?**
   Your partner opened 1 No trump.

5 **WHAT IS YOUR REBID?**
   Your partner opened 1 Diamond.
   You responded 1 Spade.
   Your partner bid 2 Clubs.

6 **WHAT IS YOUR BID?**
   Your right hand opponent opened 1 Diamond.

7 **WHAT IS YOUR BID?**
   Your left hand opponent opened 1 Heart.
   Your partner doubled.
   Your right hand opponent passed.

8 **WHAT IS YOUR BID?**
   Your partner opened 1 Heart.
   Your right hand opponent doubled.

Answers on Pages 186-87

Quiz 2

1 **WHAT IS YOUR BID?**

   Your left hand opponent opened 1 Club.
   Your partner overcalled 1 Heart.
   Your right hand opponent passed.

2 **WHAT IS YOUR OPENING BID?**

3 **WHAT IS YOUR RESPONSE?**

   Your partner opened 1 No trump.

4 **WHAT IS YOUR REBID?**

   Your partner opened 1 Heart.
   You responded 1 Spade.
   Your partner bid 2 Spades.

5 **WHAT IS YOUR BID?**

   Your left hand opponent opened 1 Club.
   Your partner overcalled 1 Diamond.
   Your right hand opponent passed.

6 **WHAT IS YOUR BID?**

   You are South. Previous bidding is shown below:

WEST	NORTH	EAST	SOUTH
1 Heart	Pass	3 Hearts	Pass
4 Hearts	Pass	Pass	?

Answers on Pages 187-88

Quiz 3

1 **WHAT IS YOUR OPENING BID?**

2 **WHAT IS YOUR RESPONSE?**
   Your partner opened 1 No trump..

3 **WHAT IS YOUR REBID?**
   Your partner opened 1 Diamond.
   You responded 1 Spade.
   Your partner bid 2 Clubs.

4 **WHAT IS YOUR RESPONSE?**
   Your partner opened 3 Clubs.

5 **WHAT IS YOUR BID?**
   Your right hand opponent opened 1 Club.

6 **WHAT IS YOUR BID?**
   Your left hand opponent opened 1 Diamond.
   Your partner overcalled 2 Clubs.
   Your right hand opponent passed.

Answers on Pages 189-90

Quiz 4

1 **WHAT IS YOUR OPENING BID?**

2 **WHAT IS YOUR RESPONSE?**
   Your partner opened 1 No trump.

3 **WHAT IS YOUR REBID?**
   You opened 1 Diamond.
   Your partner responded 1 No trump.

4 **WHAT IS YOUR REBID?**
   You opened 1 Diamond.
   Your partner responded 2 Diamonds.

5 **WHAT IS YOUR REBID?**
   You opened 1 Diamond.
   Your partner responded 1 Heart.

6 **WHAT IS YOUR BID?**
   You are South.
   Previous bidding is shown below:

SOUTH	WEST	NORTH	EAST
1 Diamond	Pass	2 Hearts	Pass
2 Spades	Pass	3 Hearts	Pass
4 Diamonds	Pass	4 Hearts	Pass
?			

Answers on Pages 190-92

Quiz 5

1 WHAT IS YOUR OPENING BID?

2 WHAT IS YOUR RESPONSE?
Your partner opened 1 Heart.

3 WHAT IS YOUR REBID?
You opened 1 Diamond.
Your partner responded 1 Heart.

4 WHAT IS YOUR BID?
Your right hand opponent opened 1 Diamond.

5 WHAT IS YOUR REBID?
You opened 1 Diamond.
Your partner responded 1 Spade.

6 WHAT IS YOUR RESPONSE?
Your partner opened 3 Hearts.

7 WHAT IS YOUR REBID?
Your partner opened 1 Spade.
You responded 2 Diamonds.
Your partner bid 2 Spades.

8 WHAT IS YOUR BID?
Your right hand opponent opened 1 Heart.

Answers on Pages 192-93

Quiz 6

1 **WHAT IS YOUR OPENING BID?**

2 **WHAT IS YOUR RESPONSE?**
   Your partner opened 1 Diamond.

3 **WHAT IS YOUR REBID?**
   You opened 1 Diamond.
   Your partner bid 1 No trump.

4 **WHAT IS YOUR RESPONSE?**
   Your partner opened 1 Club.

5 **WHAT IS YOUR BID?**
   Your right hand opponent opened 1 Diamond.

6 **WHAT IS YOUR BID?**
   You are South.
   Previous bidding is shown below:

NORTH	EAST	SOUTH	WEST
1 Spade	Pass	2 Diamonds	Pass
4 Clubs	Pass	?	

Answers on Pages 194-95

Quiz 7

1 **WHAT IS YOUR RESPONSE?**
Your partner opened 3 Clubs.

2 **WHAT IS YOUR RESPONSE?**
Your partner opened 1 Club.

3 **WHAT IS YOUR REBID?**
You opened 1 Diamond.
Your partner responded 1 Spade.

4 **WHAT IS YOUR REBID?**
You opened 1 Diamond.
Your partner responded 1 No trump.

5 **WHAT IS YOUR RESPONSE?**
Your partner opened 1 Heart.

6 **WHAT IS YOUR REBID?**
Your partner opened 1 Heart.
You responded 2 Diamonds.
Your partner bid 3 Clubs.

7 **WHAT IS YOUR REBID?**
You opened 1 Diamond.
Your partner responded 1 Heart.

Answers on Pages 195-97

Quiz 8

1 **WHAT IS YOUR OPENING BID?**

2 **WHAT IS YOUR REBID?**

  You opened 1 Spade.
  Your partner responded 2 Spades.

3 **WHAT IS YOUR REBID?**

  You opened 1 Spade.
  Your partner responded 2 Hearts.

4 **WHAT IS YOUR BID?**

  Your right hand opponent opened 1 Heart.

5 **WHAT IS YOUR REBID?**

  You are South.
  Previous bidding is shown below:

SOUTH	WEST	NORTH	EAST
1 Spade	Pass	3 Spades	Pass
?			

6 **WHAT IS YOUR REBID?**

  You opened 1 Spade.
  Your partner responded 2 Clubs.

Answers on Pages 197-98

Quiz 9

1 **WHAT IS YOUR OPENING BID?**

2 **WHAT IS YOUR RESPONSE?**
Your partner opened 1 Diamond.

3 **WHAT IS YOUR REBID?**
You opened 1 Spade.
Your partner responded 2 Spades.

4 **WHAT IS YOUR REBID?**
You opened 1 Spade.
Your partner responded 2 Clubs.

5 **WHAT IS YOUR BID?**
Your right hand opponent opened 1 Spade.

6 **WHAT IS YOUR RESPONSE?**
Your partner opened 1 Heart.

7 **WHAT IS YOUR RESPONSE?**
Your partner opened 1 No trump.

Answers on Pages 199-200

Quiz 10

1 WHAT IS YOUR OPENING BID?

2 WHAT IS YOUR RESPONSE?
Your partner opened 1 Club.

3 WHAT IS YOUR REBID?
You opened 1 Diamond.
Your partner responded 1 No trump.

4 WHAT IS YOUR REBID?
You opened 1 Diamond.
Your partner responded 2 Diamonds.

5 WHAT IS YOUR REBID?
You opened 1 Diamond.
Your partner responded 1 Spade.

Answers on Pages 201-02

Quiz 11

1 **WHAT IS YOUR OPENING BID?**

2 **WHAT IS YOUR RESPONSE?**
Your partner opened 1 Diamond.

3 **WHAT IS YOUR REBID?**
You opened 1 Heart.
Your partner responded 1 No trump.

4 **WHAT IS YOUR REBID?**
You opened 1 Heart.
Your partner responded 2 Hearts.

5 **WHAT IS YOUR REBID?**
You opened 1 Heart.
Your partner responded 1 Spade.

Answers on Pages 202-03

Quiz 12

1 **WHAT IS YOUR OPENING BID?**

2 **WHAT IS YOUR RESPONSE?**
  Your partner opened 1 Spade.

3 **WHAT IS YOUR BID?**
  Your partner opened 1 Heart.
  Your right hand opponent doubled.

4 **WHAT IS YOUR RESPONSE?**
  Your partner opened 1 No trump.

5 **WHAT IS YOUR REBID?**
  Your partner opened 1 Diamond.
  You responded 1 Spade.
  Your partner bid 2 Hearts.

6 **WHAT IS YOUR REBID?**
  Your partner opened 1 Heart.
  You responded 1 Spade.
  Your partner bid 2 Hearts.

7 **WHAT IS YOUR BID?**
  Your left hand opponent opened 1 Heart.
  Your partner doubled.
  Your right hand opponent bid 2 Hearts.

Answers on Pages 203-04

Quiz 13

1 **WHAT IS YOUR OPENING BID?**

2 **WHAT IS YOUR RESPONSE?**
Your partner opened 1 Diamond.

3 **WHAT IS YOUR RESPONSE?**
Your partner opened 1 No trump.

4 **WHAT IS YOUR RESPONSE?**
Your partner opened 2 No trump.

5 **WHAT IS YOUR BID?**
Your right hand opponent opened 1 Diamond.

6 **WHAT IS YOUR BID?**
Your left hand opponent opened 1 Heart.
Your partner doubled.
Your right hand opponent passed.

7 **WHAT IS YOUR BID?**
Your partner opened 1 Club.
Your right hand opponent overcalled 1 Diamond.

Answers on Pages 205-06

Quiz 14

1 WHAT IS YOUR OPENING BID?

2 WHAT IS YOUR REBID?
You opened 1 No trump.
Your partner responded 2 No trump.

3 WHAT IS YOUR BID?
Your right hand opponent opened 1 Diamond.

4 WHAT IS YOUR RESPONSE?
Your partner opened 3 Spades.

5 WHAT IS YOUR REBID?
You opened 1 No trump.
Your partner bid 2 Spades.

6 WHAT IS YOUR BID?
Your right hand opponent opened 1 Spade.

7 WHAT IS YOUR RESPONSE?
Your partner opened 1 No trump.

8 WHAT IS YOUR REBID?
You opened 1 No trump.
Your partner responded 4 No trump.

Answers on Pages 207-08

Quiz 15

1 WHAT IS YOUR OPENING BID?

2 WHAT IS YOUR REBID?
You opened 1 No trump.
Your partner responded 2 No trump.

3 WHAT IS YOUR BID?
Your right hand opponent opened 1 Spade.

4 WHAT IS YOUR REBID?
You opened 1 No trump.
Your partner responded 2 Spades.

5 WHAT IS YOUR REBID?
You opened 1 No trump.
Your partner responded 2 Hearts.

6 WHAT IS YOUR BID?
Your right hand opponent opened 1 Diamond.

7 WHAT IS YOUR REBID?
You opened 1 No trump.
Your partner responded 2 Diamonds.

8 WHAT IS YOUR REBID?
You opened 1 No trump.
Your partner responded 4 No trump.

Answers on Pages 208-210

Quiz 16

1 **WHAT IS YOUR OPENING BID?**

2 **WHAT IS YOUR REBID?**

You opened 1 No trump.
Your partner responded 2 Clubs.

3 **WHAT IS YOUR REBID?**

You opened 1 No trump.
Your partner responded 2 Diamonds.

4 **WHAT IS YOUR REBID?**

You opened 1 No trump.
Your partner responded 2 No trump.

5 **WHAT IS YOUR REBID?**

You opened 1 No trump.
Your partner responded 2 Hearts.

Answers on Pages 210-11

Quiz 17

1 WHAT IS YOUR RESPONSE?
Your partner opened 1 Heart.

2 WHAT IS YOUR RESPONSE?
Your partner opened 1 Diamond.

3 WHAT IS YOUR REBID?
Your partner opened 1 Diamond.
Your responded 2 Diamonds.
Your partner bid 3 Diamonds.

4 WHAT IS YOUR REBID?
Your partner opened 1 Diamond.
You responded 2 Diamonds.
Your partner bid 2 Hearts.

5 WHAT IS YOUR BID?
Your partner opened 1 Heart.
Your right hand opponent doubled.

6 WHAT IS YOUR RESPONSE?
Your partner opened 2 No trump.

7 WHAT IS YOUR REBID?
Your partner opened 1 Diamond.
You responded 2 Diamonds.
Your partner bid 2 No trump.

Answers on Pages 212-13

Quiz 18

1 **WHAT IS YOUR RESPONSE?**
   Your partner opened 1 Heart.

2 **WHAT IS YOUR RESPONSE?**
   Your partner opened 1 No trump.

3 **WHAT IS YOUR REBID?**
   Your partner opened 1 Heart.
   You responded 1 Spade.
   Your partner bid 2 No trump.

4 **WHAT IS YOUR RESPONSE?**
   Your partner opened 2 No trump.

5 **WHAT IS YOUR RESPONSE?**
   Your partner opened 1 Diamond.
   Your right hand opponent overcalled 1 Heart.

6 **WHAT IS YOUR BID?**
   Your partner opened 1 Heart.
   Your right hand opponent overcalled 1 Spade.

7 **WHAT IS YOUR REBID?**
   Your partner opened 1 Heart.
   You responded 1 Spade.
   Your partner bid 3 Hearts.

Answers on Pages 214-15

Quiz 19

1 **WHAT IS YOUR REBID?**
Your partner opened 1 Heart.
You responded 2 Hearts.
Your partner bid 3 Diamonds.

2 **WHAT IS YOUR RESPONSE?**
Your partner opened 1 Diamond.

3 **WHAT IS YOUR REBID?**
Your partner opened 1 Heart.
You responded 2 Hearts.
Your partner bid 3 Hearts.

4 **WHAT IS YOUR RESPONSE?**
Your partner opened 1 Heart.

5 **WHAT IS YOUR REBID?**
Your partner opened 1 Diamond.
You responded 1 Heart.
Your partner bid 2 Clubs.

6 **WHAT IS YOUR BID?**
Your partner opened 1 Spade.
Your right hand opponent overcalled 2 Diamonds.

7 **WHAT IS YOUR REBID?**
Your partner opened 1 Diamond.
You responded 1 Heart.
Your partner bid 3 Clubs.

Answers on Pages 215-16

Quiz 20

1 WHAT IS YOUR RESPONSE?
Your partner opened 1 Heart.

2 WHAT IS YOUR RESPONSE?
Your partner opened 1 Diamond.

3 WHAT IS YOUR REBID?
Your partner opened 1 Heart.
You responded 1 Spade.
Your partner bid 2 Clubs.

4 WHAT IS YOUR OPENING BID?
You are not vulnerable.

5 WHAT IS YOUR RESPONSE?
Your partner opened 3 Hearts.

6 WHAT IS YOUR BID?
Your right hand opponent opened 1 Heart.

7 WHAT IS YOUR BID?
Your left hand opponent opened 1 Spade.
Your partner doubled.
Your right hand opponent passed.

8 WHAT IS YOUR RESPONSE?
Your partner opened 1 No trump.

Answers on Pages 217-18

Quiz 21

1 WHAT IS YOUR RESPONSE?

Your partner opened 1 Spade.

2 WHAT IS YOUR REBID?

Your partner opened 1 Spade.
You responded 2 Diamonds.
Your partner bid 2 Spades.

3 WHAT IS YOUR OPENING BID?

You are not vulnerable.

4 WHAT IS YOUR BID?

Your right hand opponent opened 1 Heart.

5 WHAT IS YOUR BID?

Your left hand opponent opened 1 Heart.
Your partner overcalled 1 Spade.
Your right hand opponent passed.

6 WHAT IS YOUR BID?

Your partner opened 1 Club.
Your right hand opponent overcalled 1 Heart.

Answers on Pages 219-220

Quiz 22

1 WHAT IS YOUR BID?
Your left hand opponent opened 1 Club.
Your partner overcalled 1 Spade.
Your right hand opponent passed.

2 WHAT IS YOUR RESPONSE?
Your partner opened 1 Spade.

3 WHAT IS YOUR RESPONSE?
Your partner opened 1 No trump.

4 WHAT IS YOUR REBID?
Your partner opened 1 Spade.
You responded 2 Diamonds.
Your partner bid 3 Diamonds.

5 WHAT IS YOUR REBID?
Your partner opened 1 Club.
You responded 1 Diamond.
Your partner bid 1 Spade.

6 WHAT IS YOUR RESPONSE?
Your partner opened 3 Spades.

7 WHAT IS YOUR BID?
Your left hand opponent opened 1 Spade.
Your partner overcalled 2 Hearts.
Your right hand opponent passed.

Answers on Pages 220-22

Quiz 23

1 **WHAT IS YOUR REBID?**

Your partner opened 1 Spade.
You responded 2 Spades.
Your partner bid 3 Spades.

2 **WHAT IS YOUR BID?**

Your left hand opponent opened 1 Diamond.
Your partner doubled.
Your right hand opponent redoubled.

3 **WHAT IS YOUR RESPONSE?**

Your partner opened 1 Club.

4 **WHAT IS YOUR BID?**

Your left hand opponent opened 1 Diamond.
Your partner doubled.
Your right hand opponent passed.

5 **WHAT IS YOUR REBID?**

Your partner opened 1 Spade.
You responded 2 Spades.
Your partner bid 2 No trump.

6 **WHAT IS YOUR BID?**

Your partner opened 1 Heart.
Your right hand opponent overcalled 1 Spade.

Answers on Pages 222-23

Quiz 24

1 **WHAT IS YOUR RESPONSE?**
Your partner opened 1 Diamond.

2 **WHAT IS YOUR RESPONSE?**
Your partner opened 2 Spades.

3 **WHAT IS YOUR BID?**
Your left hand opponent opened 1 Club.
Your partner doubled.
Your right hand opponent bid 1 Spade.

4 **WHAT IS YOUR BID?**
Your partner opened 1 Heart.
Your right hand opponent overcalled 1 Spade.
You passed. Your left hand opponent passed.
Your partner bid 2 Diamonds.
Your right hand opponent passed.

5 **WHAT IS YOUR RESPONSE?**
Your partner opened 2 No trump.

6 **WHAT IS YOUR RESPONSE?**
Your first opponent opened 1 Club.
Your partner doubled.

7 **WHAT IS YOUR BID?**
Your left hand opponent opened 1 Club.
Your partner doubled.
Your right hand opponent redoubled.

Answers on Pages 224-25

Quiz 25

1 **WHAT IS YOUR RESPONSE?**
   Your partner opened 1 Spade.

2 **WHAT IS YOUR REBID?**
   Your partner opened 1 Heart.
   You responded 1 No trump.
   Your partner bid 3 Spades.

3 **WHAT IS YOUR REBID?**
   Your partner opened 1 Diamond.
   You responded 2 Diamonds.
   Your partner bid 2 No trump.

4 **WHAT IS YOUR RESPONSE?**
   Your partner opened 2 No trump.

5 **WHAT IS YOUR BID?**
   Your left hand opponent opened 1 Diamond.
   Your partner overcalled 2 Hearts.
   Your right hand opponent passed.

6 **WHAT IS YOUR BID?**
   Your partner opened 1 Diamond.
   Your right opponent overcalled 1 Heart.

7 **WHAT IS YOUR REBID?**
   Your partner opened 1 Spade.
   You responded 1 No trump.
   Your partner bid 2 Hearts.

Answers on Pages 225-26

Quiz 26

1 **WHAT IS YOUR RESPONSE?**
   Your partner opened 1 Heart.

2 **WHAT IS YOUR OPENING BID?**

3 **WHAT IS YOUR REBID?**
   You opened 1 Spade.
   Your partner responded 1 No trump.

4 **WHAT IS YOUR REBID?**
   You opened 1 Spade.
   Your partner responded 2 Hearts.

5 **WHAT IS YOUR BID?**
   Your right hand opponent opened 1 Heart.

Answers on Pages 227-28

Quiz 27

1 **WHAT IS YOUR OPENING BID?**

2 **WHAT IS YOUR RESPONSE?**
Your partner opened 1 Club.

3 **WHAT IS YOUR REBID?**
You opened 1 Spade.
Your partner responded 1 No trump.

4 **WHAT IS YOUR REBID?**
You opened 1 Spade.
Your partner responded 2 Spades.

5 **WHAT IS YOUR REBID?**
You opened 1 Spade.
Your partner responded 2 Clubs.

6 **WHAT IS YOUR BID?**
Your right hand opponent opened 1 Club.

7 **WHAT IS YOUR RESPONSE?**
Your partner opened 1 No trump.

Answers on Pages 228-29

Quiz 28

1 WHAT IS YOUR OPENING BID?

2 WHAT IS YOUR REBID?
You opened 1 Club.
Your partner responded 1 Spade.

3 WHAT IS YOUR RESPONSE?
Your partner opened 1 Diamond.

4 WHAT IS YOUR REBID?
You opened 1 Club.
Your partner responded 1 No trump.

5 WHAT IS YOUR REBID?
You opened 1 Club.
Your partner responded 2 Clubs.

6 WHAT IS YOUR REBID?
You opened 1 Club.
Your partner responded 1 Heart.

Answers on Pages 229-30

Quiz 29

1 **WHAT IS YOUR BID?**
Your partner opened 1 Heart.
Your right hand opponent doubled.

2 **WHAT IS YOUR RESPONSE?**
Your partner opened 1 No trump.

3 **WHAT IS YOUR REBID?**
Your partner opened 1 Heart.
You responded 1 Spade.
Your partner bid 2 Hearts.

4 **WHAT IS YOUR BID?**
Your left hand opponent opened 1 Diamond.
Your partner doubled.
Your right hand opponent bid 1 Heart.

5 **WHAT IS YOUR RESPONSE?**
Your left hand opponent opened 1 Club.
Your partner overcalled 1 Diamond.
Your right hand opponent passed.

6 **WHAT IS YOUR BID?**
Your left hand opponent opened 1 Diamond.
Your partner overcalled 2 Hearts.

7 **WHAT IS YOUR BID?**
Your left hand opponent opened 1 Heart.
Your partner doubled.
Your right opponent bid 2 Hearts.

Answers on Pages 231-32

Quiz 30

1 WHAT IS YOUR BID?
Your partner opened 1 Club.
Your right hand opponent overcalled 1 Diamond.

2 WHAT IS YOUR RESPONSE?
Your partner opened 1 No trump.

3 WHAT IS YOUR RESPONSE?
Your partner opened 2 Diamonds.

4 WHAT IS YOUR BID?
Your left hand opponent opened 1 Club.
Your partner doubled.
Your right hand opponent redoubled.

5 WHAT IS YOUR BID?
Your right hand opponent opened 1 Diamond.
You are not vulnerable.

6 WHAT IS YOUR RESPONSE?
Your left hand opponent opened 1 Diamond.
Your partner overcalled 1 No trump.
Your right hand opponent passed.

7 WHAT IS YOUR BID?
Your left hand opponent opened 1 Club.
Your partner doubled.
Your right hand opponent bid 1 Diamond.

Answers on Pages 232-34

Quiz 31

1 **WHAT IS YOUR REBID?**
Your partner opened 1 Heart.
You responded 1 Spade.
Your partner bid 2 Spades.

2 **WHAT IS YOUR BID?**
Your left hand opponent opened 1 Heart.
Your partner overcalled 2 Clubs.
Your right hand opponent passed.

3 **WHAT IS YOUR RESPONSE?**
Your partner opened 1 No trump.

4 **WHAT IS YOUR BID?**
Your right hand opponent opened 1 Club.
You are not vulnerable.

5 **WHAT IS YOUR BID?**
Your partner opened 1 Club.
Your right hand opponent overcalled 1 Heart.

6 **WHAT IS YOUR REBID?**
Your partner opened 1 Club.
You responded 1 Spade.
Your partner bid 2 Clubs.

7 **WHAT IS YOUR BID?**
Your 1st opponent opened 1 Diamond.
Your partner overcalled 1 Heart.
Your 2nd opponent passed.

Answers on Pages 234-35

Quiz 32

1 **WHAT IS YOUR BID?**
   Your right hand opponent opened 1 Spade.

2 **WHAT IS YOUR REBID?**
   You opened 1 Heart.
   Your partner responded 1 No trump.

3 **WHAT IS YOUR RESPONSE?**
   Your partner opened 3 Diamonds.

4 **WHAT IS YOUR BID?**
   Your right hand opponent opened 1 Diamond.

5 **WHAT IS YOUR BID?**
   You are South.
   Previous bidding is shown below:

NORTH	EAST	SOUTH	WEST
1 Spade	Pass	2 Hearts	Pass
4 Spades	Pass	?	

Answers on Pages 236-37

Quiz 33

1 WHAT IS YOUR RESPONSE?

Your partner opened 2 Spades.

2 WHAT IS YOUR BID?

Your left hand opponent opened 1 Diamond.
Your partner overcalled 3 Clubs.
Your right hand opponent passed.

3 WHAT IS YOUR BID?

Your partner opened 1 Spade.
Your right hand opponent doubled.

4 WHAT IS YOUR REBID?

Your partner opened 1 Spade.
You responded 1 No trump.
Your partner bid 2 No trump.

5 WHAT IS YOUR REBID?

Your partner opened 1 Spade.
You responded 1 No trump.
Your partner bid 2 Diamonds.

6 WHAT IS YOUR RESPONSE?

Your partner opened 2 Hearts.

7 WHAT IS YOUR BID?

Your partner opened 1 Heart.
Your right hand opponent overcalled 1 Spade.

Answers on Pages 237-38

Quiz 34

1 **WHAT IS YOUR OPENING BID?**

2 **WHAT IS YOUR RESPONSE?**
Your partner opened 3 Clubs.

3 **WHAT IS YOUR RESPONSE?**
Your partner opened 1 Club.

Answers on Page 239

Quiz 35

WHAT IS YOUR OPENING BID?

Answer on Page 240

Quiz 36

WHAT IS YOUR OPENING BID?

Answer on Page 240

ANSWERS TO
QUIZZES

ANSWERS TO QUIZ 1

1 2 No trump. This hand contains 12 points in high cards. Although your hand is well suited to a No trump contract, you cannot be sure of a game. Your partner may have only 13 points. His rebid of 1 No trump shows that he has a minimum opening hand. But when you hold a strong responding hand (10 to 12 points) your hand is worth at least 1 rebid. Bid 2 No trump.

2 Pass. This hand contains only 12 points in high cards. Do not make an opening bid. Moreover, you do not have a good rebid. You do not have a rebiddable suit or two biddable suits.

3 1 Spade. This hand contains 12 points in high cards. Do not respond 2 No trump. For a jump response in No trump you should have a very strong responding hand (13 to 15 points) in high cards only and strength in all unbid suits. You do not have 13 points nor do you have strength in Clubs.
The only bid you can make is 1 Spade.

4 3 No trump. This hand contains 12 points in high cards. It is a balanced hand.
With 10 to 14 points and a balanced hand, respond 3 No trump.

However, if you know that your partner is an advanced player and that he uses the 2 Club Convention, respond 2 Clubs to show that your hand contains 8 or more points and a 4 card or longer major suit.

5 3 Diamonds. This hand contains 12 points in high cards. If you hold a strong responding hand (10 to 12 points) your hand is worth at least 1 rebid.
You prefer Diamonds to Clubs. Do not bid 2 Diamonds. A bid of 2 Diamonds would show a mere preference, not a true raise.

6   Pass. This hand contains 12 points in high cards.
    With 10 to 12 points you can make a minimum over-
    call, provided you have a strong rebiddable trump suit.
    You do not have a rebiddable suit.
    Do not overcall in a four-card suit.
    Do not overcall 1 No trump, unless you have the re-
    quirements for an opening bid of 1 No trump.

7   2 Spades. This hand contains 12 points in high cards.
    With 12 points opposite your partner's take-out double
    you can probably make a game. With a strong respond-
    ing hand (10 to 12 points) and a biddable suit make a
    jump response. Bid 2 Spades, 1 more than necessary.
    This response is better than a bid of 1 No trump, be-
    cause you have such a good Spade suit.

8   Redouble. This hand contains 12 points in high cards.
    When your partner opens the bidding and your right
    hand opponent makes a take-out double, redouble if
    you have a strong responding hand (10 to 12 points).

ANSWERS TO QUIZ 2

1   2 Hearts. This hand contains 12 points—11 points in
    high cards and 1 point for the doubleton.
    With a strong responding hand (10 to 12 points) and
    sufficient trump support, you can raise your partner's
    minimum overcall. One less trump is required to raise
    an overcall than is required to raise an opening bid.

2   Pass. This hand contains 12 points—11 in high cards
    and 1 point for the doubleton.
    With only 12 points you can not make an opening bid.

3   3 Spades. This hand contains 12 points—11 in high cards and 1 additional point, because the hand contains a five-card suit.

When your partner has opened 1 No trump, and you have the points necessary for a raise to 3 No trump (10 to 14 points) and you also have a long, strong suit, you can give a jump response in that suit. This jump response is forcing to game.

4   4 Spades. This hand contains 12 points—11 points in high cards and 1 point for the doubleton. However, after your partner has raised your Spades, you may count an additional point for the fifth Spade. Therefore, your hand is really worth 13 points after it has been revalued. Even if your partner has only 13 points, you have 26 points in the combined hands. With your partner's support in Spades you can make the game.

5   1 Spade. This hand contains 12 points—11 points in high cards and 1 point for the doubleton.

With a strong responding hand (10 to 12 points), you can respond to your partner's minimum overcall by bidding a rebiddable suit of your own at the same level or by raising your partner's suit (if you have the necessary trump support).

Usually it is better to raise your partner's overcall than to bid your own suit. But in this case it is better to show your strong rebiddable major suit than to raise your partner's minor suit.

6   Pass. This hand contains 12 points—11 points in high cards and 1 point for the doubleton.

You cannot count on your partner for any tricks. You cannot reasonably hope to take more than 3 tricks in your own hand—2 tricks in Spades and 1 trick in Hearts. This is not enough to set the contract 2 tricks.

ANSWERS TO QUIZ 3

1 Pass. This hand contains 12 points—11 points in high cards and 1 point for the doubleton.
Do not make an opening bid.

2 3 No trump. This hand contains 12 points—11 points in high cards and 1 additional point because the hand contains a five-card suit. It is a balanced hand.
With 10 to 14 points and a balanced hand, respond 3 No trump.

However, if you know that your partner is an advanced player and that he uses the 2 Club Convention, respond 2 Clubs to show that your hand contains 8 or more points and a 4 card or longer major suit.

3 2 No trump. This hand contains 11 points in high cards. Your partner's rebid indicates that he has a minimum opening hand (13 to 15 points). There is a chance that he has 15 points and that you and your partner together have 26 points.
At any rate, with a strong responding hand (10 to 12 points), your hand is worth at least 1 rebid.

4 Pass. This hand contains 12 points—11 points in high cards and 1 point for the doubleton.
This hand does not have enough points for a response to a preemptive opening bid of 3 in a suit. To respond you must have a very strong responding hand (13 to 15 points).
But even if you had 13 to 15 points you could not respond. You could not bid 3 Spades, because you do not have a strong rebiddable Spade suit. You could not bid 3 No trump, because you do not have 1 of the 3 top honors in your partner's minor suit.

ANSWERS TO QUIZ 3

5 Pass. This hand contains 12 points—11 points in high cards and 1 point for the doubleton.

To make a minimum overcall, you must hold at least 10 to 12 points. But the number of high points you hold is less important than the kind of suit you hold. To make an overcall, you must have a rebiddable suit.

Your Spade suit is too weak for an overcall. Moreover, you do not want to encourage your partner to lead Spades.

6 3 Clubs. This hand contains 12 points—11 points in high cards and 1 point for the doubleton.

With a strong responding hand (10 to 12 points), you can raise your partner's minimum overcall if you have adequate support in trumps. Adequate trump support for an overcall requires 1 trump less than adequate support for an opening bid.

If you can raise your partner's overcall, do not show a suit of your own, unless you have a strong rebiddable suit.

Your Spade suit is too weak to show. Your partner may not have any support for your Spades.

ANSWERS TO QUIZ 4

1 1 Diamond. This hand contains 13 points—11 points in high cards and 1 point for each doubleton.

You have a convenient rebid. If your partner responds 1 Heart, you can make a rebid of 1 Spade. If your partner responds 2 Clubs, you can bid 2 Diamonds.

If you hold 2 suits of unequal length, bid the longer suit first.

ANSWERS TO QUIZ 4

2   3 Diamonds. This hand contains 12 points in response to an opening bid of 1 No trump—11 points in high cards and 1 additional point for a five-card suit.

When you hold a good five-card or longer suit and also have the requirements for a raise to 3 No trump (10 to 14 points), you may jump to 3 in your suit. This jump response is forcing to game.

However, if you know that your partner is an advanced player and that he uses the 2 Club Convention, respond 2 Clubs to show that your hand contains 8 or more points and a 4 card or longer major suit.

3   2 Diamonds. This hand contains 13 points—11 points in high cards and 1 point for each doubleton.

Obviously there is no hope for a game. But this is an unbalanced hand which may play better at a suit. It may be safer to play this hand at a 2 Diamond contract rather than a 1 No trump contract.

When you open the bidding with a minimum opening hand (13 to 15 points), and your partner responds 1 No trump, rebid only for the sake of safety.

4   Pass. This hand contains 13 points—11 points in high cards and 1 point for each doubleton. After your partner has raised your Diamonds, you can add 1 additional point for the fifth Diamond. Therefore, your revalued hand is worth 14 points.

If your revalued hand is still classified as a minimum opening hand (13 to 15 points), do not rebid after your partner has given you a single raise.

5   1 Spade. This hand contains 13 points—11 points on high cards and 1 point for each doubleton.

When you rebid in a new suit at the level of 1, you show that you have a minimum opening hand (13 to 15 points). This bid allows your partner to return to Diamonds, your original suit, at the level of 2.

ANSWERS TO QUIZ 4

6 Pass. This hand contains 12 points in support of Hearts —11 points in high cards and 1 point for the doubleton Club. You cannot count 1 point for the doubleton in trumps.

Your partner's jump response in a new suit indicates that he has a tremendous responding hand (19 to 21 points). But you can only be sure of 31 points in the combined hands. A small slam requires 33 points.

ANSWERS TO QUIZ 5

1 1 Diamond. This hand contains 14 points—13 points in hard cards and 1 point for the doubleton.

With 14 points you must open. With 2 suits of equal length, bid the higher ranking suit first.

2 2 No trump. This hand contains 13 points in high cards. It is a balanced hand. For a jump response of 2 No trump, you must have a very strong responding hand (13 to 15 points) in high cards and strength in all the unbid suits. You must have a balanced hand. With a balanced hand, you will have at least 2 of your partner's suit.

A jump response of 2 No trump is forcing to game.

3 1 No trump. This hand contains 14 points—13 points in high cards and 1 point for the doubleton.

When you bid 1 No trump, you tell your partner that you have a minimum opening hand (13 to 15 points). You also show that you have a balanced hand.

ANSWERS TO QUIZ 5

4 Pass. This hand contains 14 points—13 points in high cards and 1 point for the doubleton.

You cannot make a take-out double, because you do not have adequate support for Hearts. You cannot overcall 1 No trump, because your hand is not strong enough. You cannot make an overcall in a suit, because you do not have a rebiddable suit.

5 2 Spades. This hand contains 14 points—13 points in high cards and 1 point for the doubleton.

This is a minimum opening hand (13 to 15 points). Even with a minimum opening hand, you can raise your partner's major suit from 1 to 2, if you have adequate trump support.

6 4 Hearts. This hand contains 13 points in high cards. Do not count 1 point for the doubleton in your partner's Heart suit.

You do not need trump support to raise an opening pre-emptive bid of 3 in a suit. However, you do need a very strong responding hand (13 to 15 points).

7 4 Spades. This hand contains 14 points—13 points in high cards and 1 point for the doubleton.

You have a very strong responding hand (13 to 15 points). Nevertheless, you cannot bid 3 Spades on your first response, because you do not have enough trumps for a double raise. Your 2 Diamond responce forces your partner to bid again and assures you a second chance to bid. After your partner has rebid his Spades, you can jump to 4 Spades. Even though your partner has a minimum opening hand (13 to 15 points), you have at least 26 points in the combined hands.

8 Double. This hand contains 14 points—13 points in high cards and 1 point for the doubleton.

If you have 13 to 15 points or more and adequate trump support for any suit in which your partner may respond, you have an ideal hand for a take-out double.

ANSWERS TO QUIZ 6

1 1 Diamond. This hand contains 14 points in high cards. Whenever your hand contains 14 points you must open. Do not bid 1 No trump. A strong opening hand (16 to 18 points) is required for an opening bid of 1 No trump.

2 3 Diamonds. This hand contains 14 points in high cards. For a double raise you must have 1 trump more than required for normal trump support. You must also have a very strong responding hand (13 to 15 points). Do not respond 2 No trump, because you do not have strength in Clubs.

3 Pass. This hand contains 14 points in high cards.
There is no hope for a game, and your hand is well suited to a No trump contract.
When you open the bidding with a minimum opening hand (13 to 15 points), and your partner responds 1 No trump, rebid only for safety.

4 2 No trump. This hand contains 14 points in high cards. With a very strong responding hand (13 to 15 points) in high cards, and strength in all unbid suits, you can respond 2 No trump. You have all these requirements. Do not respond 2 Diamonds when you can respond 2 No trump.

5 Pass. This hand contains 14 points in high cards.
You cannot make a take-out double, because you do not have adequate support for Clubs. You cannot bid 1 No trump because your hand is not strong enough. You cannot make an overcall in a suit, because you do not have a rebiddable suit.

ANSWERS TO QUIZ 6

6 4 No trump. This hand contains 14 points in high cards. Your partner's jump rebid in a new suit indicates that he has a powerful opening hand (22 points or more). You certainly have more than 33 points in the combined hands. You have ample points for a slam in No trump. Therefore, find out about the Aces by using the Blackwood convention. Bid 4 No trump. If your partner's response shows that he holds 2 Aces, bid 5 No trump to find out about the Kings.

ANSWERS TO QUIZ 7

1 3 No trump. This hand contains 17 points—15 points in high cards and 1 point for each doubleton.

When your partner opens with a bid of 3 in a minor suit, if you have a very strong responding hand (13 to 15 points) with Ax, Kx, or Qx in your partner's suit, you can respond 3 No trump.

Do not raise your partner's minor suit.

2 1 Diamond. This hand contains 17 points—15 points in high cards and 1 point for each doubleton.

If your partner rebids 1 No trump, 1 Spade, or 2 Clubs, you can show the strength of your hand by making a jump rebid in Hearts.

Do not respond 2 No trump. You do not have strength in Spades. Do not respond 2 Hearts or 3 Diamonds. You need a tremendous responding hand (19 to 21 points) for a jump response in a new suit.

ANSWERS TO QUIZ 7

3   2 Hearts. This hand contains 17 points—15 points in high cards and 1 point for each doubleton.

Your rebid of 2 in a suit higher ranking than your first suit makes it impossible for your partner to return to your original Diamond suit at the level of 2. Therefore, it tells your partner that you have a strong opening hand (16 to 18 points).

Do not bid 2 No trump, because you do not have balanced distribution.

4   Pass. This hand contains 17 points—15 points in high cards and 1 point for each doubleton.

Do not rebid. Even with a strong opening hand (16 to 18 points) you should rebid only for safety. Your hand is fairly well suited to No trump play. You need not rebid for safety.

5   2 Diamonds. This hand contains 17 points—15 points in high cards and 1 point for each doubleton.

With a very strong responding hand (13 to 15 points) and 1 trump more than adequate support you can give a double raise in your partner's suit. But a double raise is limited to hands of this class (13 to 15 points). This hand is too strong for a double raise.

A response of 2 Diamonds forces your partner to keep the bidding open one round. You can show your strength on your first rebid.

6   4 Hearts. This hand contains 17 points—15 points in high cards and 1 point for each doubleton.

With a powerful responding hand (16 to 18 points), you can show your strength by bidding a new suit on your first response and then making a jump on your rebid. With four-card support for your partner you can jump in his suit.

This jump to game is not a sign-off bid.

ANSWERS TO QUIZ 7

7 3 Hearts. This hand contains 17 points—15 points in high cards and 1 point for each doubleton.

This hand is too strong for a raise to 2 Hearts. A rebid in your partner's suit at the level of 2 would indicate that you have a minimum opening hand (13 to 15 points).

With a strong opening hand (16 to 18 points) and four of your partner's suit you should raise to 3 in partner's suit, even though a jump rebid is necessary to reach that level.

ANSWERS TO QUIZ 8

1 1 Spade. This hand contains 17 points—16 points in high cards and 1 point for the doubleton. It is a balanced hand.

You cannot bid 1 No trump, because your doubleton is not headed by K or better.

2 3 Spades. This hand contains 17 points—16 points in high cards and 1 point for the doubleton. However, after your partner has raised your Spades, you can revalue your hand, counting 1 additional point for the fifth Spade. Therefore your hand is really worth 18 points after it is revalued.

Since your partner can give you a single raise with as little as 6 points, you cannot be sure that there is a game in the hand. However, by bidding 3 Spades you can invite him to bid again, if he has 8 or more points.

When you have opened the bidding and your partner has given you a single raise, if you have a strong opening hand (16 to 18 points), rebid, but do not jump.

ANSWERS TO QUIZ 8

3 3 Hearts. This hand contains 17 points—16 points in high cards and 1 point for the doubleton.

With a strong opening hand (16 to 18 points), you have strength enough to raise your partner to the level of 3. Do not bid 2 Spades. A rebid in your own suit at the level of 2 would indicate that you have a minimum opening hand (13 to 15 points).

4 Double. This hand contains 17 points—16 points in high cards and 1 point for the doubleton.

Even though you do not have adequate support for Clubs, you may make a take-out double with 13 to 15 points, because you have a strong, rebiddable Spade suit which you can safely bid if your partner responds in Clubs.

Do not bid 1 No trump. Your doubleton in Clubs is not headed by K or better.

5 4 Spades. This hand contains 17 points—16 points in high cards and 1 point for the doubleton. However, after your partner has raised your Spades, you can count 1 additional point for your fifth Spade. Therefore, your hand is really worth 18 points after it is revalued.

Your partner's jump response indicates that he holds a very strong responding hand (13 to 15 points). However, it does not gurantee more than 13. Therefore, you have no assurance that you have 33 points in the combined hands. Even though you have a powerful Spade suit, you have not found a strong side suit.

Therefore, do not try for slam.

6 2 No trump. This hand contains 17 points—16 points in high cards and 1 point for the doubleton.

A rebid in Spades on the level of 2 would indicate that you have a minimum opening hand (13 to 15 points). This hand is too strong for such a weak rebid.

A bid of 2 No trump shows that you hold a strong opening hand (16 to 18 points) in high cards and a balanced hand.

ANSWERS TO QUIZ 9

1 1 Spade. This hand contains 18 points in high cards. It is a balanced hand. Three suits are stopped.

Do not bid 1 No trump, because your doubleton is not headed by K or better.

With 2 suits of equal length, bid the higher ranking suit first.

2 2 Spades. This hand contains 19 points—18 points in high cards and 1 point for the doubleton.

With a tremendous responding hand (19 to 21 points) and 4 of your partner's suit, you can give a jump response in a new suit, even though you do not have a long, strong suit.

This jump response in a new suit is an invitation to try for a slam.

3 2 No trump. This hand contains 18 points in high cards. After a single raise by your partner, if you have a strong opening hand (16 to 18 points) in high cards and a balanced hand, rebid in No trump, but do not jump.

Your hand is well suited to a No trump contract. Your bid of 2 No trump invites your partner to bid again, if he has 8 or more points. Let your partner decide whether the hand should be played at Spades or No trump.

4 2 No trump. This hand contains 18 points in high cards. Your partner's response shows that he has a strong responding hand (10 to 12 points). Therefore, you have better than 26 points in the combined hands and game is certain. However, do not jump to 3 No trump. After a "two over one" response, a jump to 3 No trump would indicate that you have a very strong opening hand (19 to 21 points) in high cards.

You need not fear that you will be left at 2 No trump. Your partner will bid again.

ANSWERS TO QUIZ 9

5 Double. This hand contains 18 points in high cards.
You have more than the 13 to 15 points required for a
take-out double. Even though you do not have adequate
support for Clubs, you can make a take-out double,
because your Spades are so strong that you can bid No
trump if your partner responds in Clubs.

Do not bid 1 No trump, because your doubleton is not
headed by K or better.

Do not overcall in a 4-card suit.

6 1 Spade. This hand contains 19 points—18 points in
high cards and 1 point for the doubleton.
You have a tremendous responding hand (19 to 21
points), but you do not have a long, strong suit or 4 of
your partner's suit. Therefore, do not make a jump response in a new suit. Your bid of 1 Spade forces your
partner to bid again. You can show your strength on
your first rebid.

7 6 No trump. This hand contains 18 points in high cards.
If you hold 17 or 18 points in high cards, jump to slam,
because you know that your partner has at least 16
points in his own hand.

ANSWERS TO QUIZ 10

1 1 Diamond. This hand contains 22 points—21 in high cards and 1 point for the doubleton.

With 14 points you must open. With 2 suits of equal length, bid the higher ranking suit first.

Do not open 1 No trump, because you have more than 18 points in high cards.

Do not open 2 No trump, because you do not have the required 22 to 24 points in high cards.

Do not open 2 in a suit. You do not have a long, strong trump suit, nor do you have enough points.

2 2 Diamonds. This hand contains 22 points—21 points in high cards and 1 point for the doubleton.

With a tremendous responding hand (19 to 21 points) or more and 4 of your partner's suit, make a jump response in a new suit, even though you do not have a long, strong suit.

This jump response in a new suit forces your partner to keep the bidding open until game is reached. It invites a slam.

3 3 No trump. This hand contains 21 points in high cards. Your partner's response of 1 No trump shows that he has a minimum responding hand (6 to 9 points) in high cards. Therefore, you have more than the 26 points in high cards required to make a game in No trump.

When you open bidding 1 in a suit and your partner responds 1 No trump, if you have a very strong opening hand (19 to 21 points) or more, jump to game, or force your partner to keep the bidding open until game is reached by making a jump rebid in a new suit.

ANSWERS TO QUIZ 10

4 3 No trump. This hand contains 22 points—21 points in high cards and 1 point for the doubleton.

When your partner gives you a single raise in your suit, if you have a very strong opening hand (19 to 21 points) or more, jump to game or force your partner to keep the bidding open until game is reached by making a jump rebid in a new suit.

With a hand so well suited to a No trump contract, jump to game in No trump.

5 3 No trump. This hand contains 22 points—21 points in high cards and 1 point for the doubleton. It is strong enough for a jump rebid in a new suit. However, it is so well suited to No trump play that a jump to 3 No trump is better. A jump bid of 3 No trump after a "one over one" response requires a powerful opening hand (22 points and up).

You do not sign off when you jump to 3 No trump. You invite your partner to explore a slam, if he has a strong responding hand.

ANSWERS TO QUIZ 11

1 1 Heart. This hand contains 22 points—19 points in high cards, 1 point for the doubleton, and 2 points for the singleton.

With 14 or more points you must open. With 2 suits of equal length, bid the higher ranking suit first.

Do not open 2 in a suit. For an opening bid of 2 in a suit you need 25 points with 1 strong five-card suit or 24 points with 2 strong five-card suits.

ANSWERS TO QUIZ 11

2 2 Hearts. This hand contains 22 points—19 points in high cards, 1 point for the doubleton, and 2 points for the singleton.

With a tremendous responding hand (19 to 21 points) or more, and a strong suit of your own, you can make a jump response in a new suit. This jump response in a new suit forces your partner to keep the bidding open until game is reached, and invites a slam.

3 3 Clubs. This hand contains 22 points—19 points in high cards, 1 point for the doubleton, and 2 points for the singleton.

When your partner responds with 1 No trump, if you hold a powerful opening hand (22 points and up), either jump to game or force your partner to keep the bidding open until game is reached by making a jump rebid in a new suit.

4 4 Clubs. This hand contains 22 points—19 points in high cards, 1 point for the doubleton, and 2 points for the singleton.

When your partner responds with a single raise in your suit, if you hold a powerful opening hand (22 points and up), either jump to game or force your partner to keep the bidding open until game is reached by making a jump rebid in a new suit.

5 3 Clubs. This hand contains 22 points—19 points in high cards, 1 point for the doubleton, and 2 points for the singleton.

With a powerful opening hand (22 points and up), make a jump rebid in a new suit. This forces your partner to keep the bidding open until game is reached. It invites a slam.

ANSWERS TO QUIZ 12

1 Pass. This hand contains 11 points—10 points in high cards and 1 point for the doubleton.
   You should have at least 13 points for an opening bid of 1 in a suit.

2 2 Clubs. This hand contains 11 points—10 points in high cards and 1 point for the doubleton.
   With a strong responding hand (10 to 12 points) and a biddable suit, you can respond "two over one."
   Bid 2 Clubs. If your partner rebids Spades, raise him to 3 Spades.

3 Redouble. This hand contains 11 points—10 points in high cards and 1 point for the doubleton.
   A redouble shows that you have a strong responding hand (10 to 12 points).
   You do not need support for your partner in order to redouble.
   If you have a strong responding hand (10 to 12 points), you should redouble rather than make a bid of your own.

4 3 No trump. This hand contains 10 points in high cards. It is a balanced hand.
   With a balanced hand and 10 to 14 points, jump to 3 No trump.
   However, if you know that your partner is an advanced player and that he uses the 2 Club Convention, respond 2 Clubs to show that your hand contains 8 or more points and a 4 card or longer major suit.

5 2 No trump. This hand contains 11 points—10 points in high cards and 1 point for the doubleton.
   When you hold a strong responding hand (10 to 12 points), your hand is worth 2 bids.
   Rebid 2 No trump rather than 3 Clubs. Your hand is well suited to a No trump contract.

6 3 Clubs. This hand contains 11 points—10 points in high cards and 1 point for the doubleton.

With a strong responding hand (10 to 12 points), your hand is worth two bids. Your partner may have 15 points, so keep the bidding open. If your partner should bid 3 Spades, showing a mere preference and not a true raise, then pass. Do not try for game.

7 2 Spades. This hand contains 11 points—10 points in high cards and 1 point for the doubleton.

When your right hand opponent inserts a bid after a take-out double by your partner, you are not forced to bid. If you bid in this situation, you show that you have a minimum responding hand (6 to 9 points) or more.

You have enough strength to bid your Spades even at the level of 2.

ANSWERS TO QUIZ 13

1 Pass. This hand contains 5 points—3 points for high cards and 2 points for the singleton.

Do not bid 1 Heart, because you do not have 12 points. Do not bid 3 Hearts, because you do not have approximately 10 points.

2 Pass. This hand contains 5 points—3 points for high cards and 2 points for the singleton.

Do not respond 1 No trump with less than a minimum responding hand (6 to 9 points) in high cards.

Do not respond "one over one" with less than a minimum responding hand (6 to 9 points), counting points both for high cards and for short suits.

3 2 Hearts. This hand contains 4 points—3 points in high cards and 1 point for the six-card suit.
Even though you have less than 8 points, you can respond 2 in a suit if you have a weak hand that contains a long, safe suit in which the hand obviously can be played safely.

4 3 Hearts. This hand contains 3 points in high cards.
When you count up your points before responding to a bid of 2 No trump, do not count points for short suits. If you have a six-card major suit, respond even though the hand contains no points in high cards.

5 Pass. This hand contains 5 points—3 points in high cards and 2 points for the singleton.
Although you have a Heart suit strong enough for an overcall, you do not have enough points. For a minimum overcall you should have 10 to 12 points or more.

6 Pass. This hand contains 5 points—3 points for high cards and 2 points for the singleton.
When your partner makes a take-out double, pass only when you have great length and strength in opponents' suit and expect to set the contract.
Your partner's take-out double indicates that he can take 3 tricks. You must be able to take the additional 4 tricks necessary to set the contract. At least 3 of your tricks should be in the trump suit.

7 Pass. This hand contains 5 points—3 points for high cards and 2 points for the singleton.
Your hand is too weak for a free bid. A free response requires more than the bare minimum number of points required for a normal "one over one" response. Even at the level of 1 you should have 9 or 10 points for a free response in a new suit.

ANSWERS TO QUIZ 14

1 1 No trump. This hand contains 16 points in high cards. It is a strong opening hand (16 to 18 points). It has balanced distribution. The doubleton is headed by the K. At least 3 suits are stopped.

This hand meets all the requirements for an opening bid of No trump.

2 Pass. This hand contains 16 points in high cards. It is a minimum opening No trump hand.

If you have a bare minimum No trump hand (16 points), you must not rebid, unless you are forced to do so.

You must pass when your partner responds 2 No trump or 2 in a suit.

3 Double. This hand contains 17 points—16 points in high cards and 1 point for the doubleton.

With 13 to 15 points or more and adequate trump support for all suits except the suit bid by your opponent, you have the requirements for a take-out double.

Do not bid 1 No trump. If the A of Diamonds is held by the opponent on your left, your Kx in your opponents' suit may not stop the Diamonds.

4 4 Spades. This hand contains 17 points—16 points in high cards and 1 point for the doubleton.

With a very strong responding hand (13 to 15 points) or more, you can raise your partner's preemptive bid of 3 in a major suit.

Do not try to slam without 3 Aces, or 2 Aces and the K or Q of your partner's suit.

5 Pass. This hand contains 16 points in high cards. It is a minimum opening No trump hand.

If you have a bare minimum No trump hand (16 point), you must not rebid unless you are forced to do so.

ANSWERS TO QUIZ 14

6 1 No trump. This hand contains 16 points in high cards. It is a strong opening hand (16 to 18 points). It has balanced distribution. It has all suits stopped. The doubleton is headed by the K.

This hand meets all the requirements for an opening bid of 1 No trump and has a stopper in opponent's Spade suit. Therefore you may overcall 1 No trump.

Do not make a take-out double. You do not have adequate support for Diamonds.

7 4 No trump. This hand contains 16 points in high cards. Invite your partner to bid a slam. You know that he has at least 16 points in his own hand.

8 Pass. This hand contains 16 points in high cards. If you have only 16 points, do not go on to slam even though your partner invites you to do so.

ANSWERS TO QUIZ 15

1 1 No trump. This hand contains 17 points in high cards. It is a strong opening hand (16 to 18 points). It has balanced distribution. The doubleton is headed by the K. All 4 suits are stopped. This hand meets all the requirements for an opening bid of 1 No trump.

2 3 Hearts. This hand contains 17 points in high cards.
It is not a bare minimum opening No trump hand (16 points). Therefore, it should be rebid. When your partner responds 2 No trump, pass only if you have a bare minimum opening No trump hand (16 points). If you and your partner each hold 4 in one of the major suits, it is safer to play for game in that suit than in No trump.
Therefore, a rebid of 3 in a four-card major is preferred to a rebid of 3 No trump. If your partner does not have 4 in your major suit, he will bid 3 No trump.

3 1 No trump. This hand contains 17 points in high cards. It is a strong opening hand (16 to 18 points). It has balanced distribution. The doubleton is headed by the K. All 4 suits are stopped. This hand meets all the requirements for an opening bid of 1 No trump and has a sure stopper in your opponents' suit. Therefore you should overcall 1 No trump.

4 Pass. This hand contains 17 points in high cards. When your partner responds 2 in a suit, do not rebid unless you have 18 points (a maximum opening No trump hand) as well as strong trump support for your partner's suit.

5 Pass. This hand contains 17 points in high cards. When your partner responds 2 in a suit, do not rebid unless you have 18 points (a maximum opening No trump hand) as well as strong trump support for your partner's suit.

6 Double. This hand contains 18 points—17 points in high cards and 1 point for the doubleton.

With 13 to 15 points or more and adequate trump support for all suits except the one bid by your opponent, you have all the requirements for a take-out double.

Do not bid 1 No trump. If the A of Diamonds is held by the opponent on your left, your Kx in Diamonds may not turn out to be a stopper in the Diamond suit.

7 Pass. This hand contains 17 points in high cards.

Since this is not a maximum No trump hand (18 points), you must pass when your partner responds 2 in a suit.

8 6 No trump. This hand contains 17 points in high cards. When your partner responds 4 No trump, jump to slam if you have 17 or 18 points.

ANSWERS TO QUIZ 16

1 1 No trump. This hand contains 18 points in high cards. It is a strong opening hand (16 to 18 points). It is a balanced hand.

It has all 4 suits stopped.

It meets all the requirements for an opening bid of 1 No trump.

2 3 Clubs. This hand contains 18 points in high cards. It is a maximum opening No trump hand. After you have made an opening bid of 1 No trump, if your partner responds with 2 in a suit, do not rebid unless you have a maximum opening No trump hand (18 points) and also have strong trump support for your partner's suit. With a maximum hand and 3 of partner's suit, including 2 of the 3 top honors, raise partner's suit to 3.

However, if you know that your partner is an advanced player who uses the 2-Club Convention, bid 2 Hearts to show that you have a 4-card Heart suit.

ANSWERS TO QUIZ 16

3 Pass. This hand contains 18 points in high cards.

When your partner responds 2 in a suit, do not rebid unless you have 18 points (a maximum opening No trump hand) and also have strong trump support for your partner's suit. You have only minimum trump support for your partner's Diamond suit. Do not bid 2 Hearts or 2 No trump.

4 3 Hearts. This hand contains 18 points in high cards.

When your partner responds with 2 No trump, you must rebid, unless you have a bare minimum opening No trump hand (16 points).

When you and your partner each hold 4 cards in the same major suit, you will usually find that a contract of 4 in that suit is a safer contract than 3 No trump. Therefore, a rebid of 3 in a four-card major is preferred to a rebid of 3 No trump. If your partner does not have 4 in your major suit, he will bid 3 No trump.

5 3 Hearts. This hand contains 18 points in high cards.

When your partner responds 2 in a suit, rebid if you have 18 points (a maximum opening No trump hand) and also have strong trump support for your partner's suit.

ANSWERS TO QUIZ 17

1 Pass. This hand contains 6 Points—5 points in high cards and 1 point for the doubleton.

You cannot make a "two over one" response, because you do not have a strong responding hand (10 to 12 points).

You cannot give a single raise, because you do not have adequate trump support.

You cannot respond 1 No trump, because you have only 5 points in high cards. In No trump bidding no points are counted for short suits.

2 2 Diamonds. This hand contains 6 points—5 points in high cards and 1 point for the doubleton.

With Qxx you have adequate trump support for your partner's Diamonds.

If you have adequate trump support, a single raise can be given with a minimum responding hand (6 to 9 points).

3 Pass. This hand contains 6 Points—5 points in high cards and 1 point for the doubleton.

After your partner has rebid, if you hold only 6 or 7 points, do not rebid unless forced to do so.

4 3 Diamonds. This hand contains 6 points as dummy for your partner's Diamond suit—5 points in high cards and 1 point for the doubleton.

When your partner has opened the bidding with 1 in a suit and on his rebid has named a second suit, you must show which of his two suits you prefer. You should select the suit in which you have the most trumps.

With this hand, you are forced to bid again in order to return to your partner's Diamond suit.

ANSWERS TO QUIZ 17

5   Pass. This hand contains 6 points—5 points in high
      cards and 1 point for the doubleton.
      With less than 10 points, ignore the double and respond
      as though your opponent had passed.
      You cannot make a "two over one" response, because
      you do not have a strong responding hand (10 to 12
      points).
      You cannot give a single raise, because you do not have
      adequate trump support.
      You cannot respond 1 No trump, because you have only
      5 points in high cards. In No trump bidding no points
      are counted for short suits.

6   3 No trump. This hand contains 5 points in high cards.
      It is a balanced hand.
      When your partner opens with 2 No trump, raise to 3
      No trump with 4 points and a balanced hand.

7   Pass. This hand contains 6 points—5 points in high
      cards and I point for the doubleton. If the hand is to be
      played at No trump, it is worth only 5 points, since no
      points are counted for short suits.
      Your partner's rebid of 2 No trump is not forcing. With
      only 6 or 7 points, you should not rebid unless you are
      forced to do so.
      With only 3 of your partner's Diamonds and with a
      balanced hand, do not go back to Diamonds.

ANSWERS TO QUIZ 18

1 1 Spade. This hand contains 7 points—5 points for high cards and 2 points for the singleton.

Do not respond 1 No trump, because you do not have a minimum responding hand (6 to 9 points) in high cards.

Do not pass, however. You can make a "one over one" response with a minimum responding hand (6 to 9 points) if you have a biddable suit.

2 Pass. This hand contains 6 points in response to an opening bid of 1 No trump—5 points in high cards and 1 additional point for the five-card suit.

With less than 8 points, there is no game in the hand.

Your Spade suit is so weak that it should not be shown.

3 Pass. This hand contains 7 points—5 points in high cards and 2 points for the singleton.

Your first response showed the full strength of your hand.

A jump rebid in No trump by the opening bidder does not force you to bid again.

With only 6 or 7 points, do not rebid, unless your partner forces you to do so.

4 3 Spades. This hand contains 5 points in high cards. In responding to No trump bids, no points are counted for short suits.

When your partner opens 2 No trump, bid any five-card major suit, if your hand contains 4 points in high cards.

5 Pass. This hand contains 7 points—5 points for high cards and 2 points for the singleton.

If your right hand opponent had passed, you would have responded 1 Spade. But your hands is too weak for a free response. A free response requires more points than the minimum number of points required for a normal "one over one" response. Even at the level of 1, a free response should not be made with less than 9 points.

ANSWERS TO QUIZ 18

6 Double. This hand contains 7 points—5 points in high cards and 2 points for the singleton.

If your right hand opponent had not overcalled, you would have responded 1 Spade.

When your partner opens the bidding, sometimes your right hand opponent overcalls in the suit you wanted to bid. In this case you should double without hesitation, unless the doubled contract, if not defeated, will give your opponents a game.

7 Pass. This hand contains 5 points in high cards as dummy for your partner's Heart suit. Do not count any points for the singleton in your partner's Heart suit.

Your first response showed the full strength of your hand. A jump rebid by the opening bidder in his original suit does not force you to bid again.

With less than 8 points, do not rebid, unless your partner forces you to do so.

———————

ANSWERS TO QUIZ 19

1 4 Hearts. This hand contains 8 points as dummy in support of your partner's Heart suit—7 points in high cards and 1 point for the doubleton.

Your partner's rebid of 3 Diamonds indicates that he has a strong opening hand (16 to 18 points) and invites you to go on to game, if you have a good strong raise. With 8 or 9 points and more than adequate trump support, jump to 4 Hearts.

2 I Heart. This hand contains 8 points—7 points in high cards and 1 point for the doubleton.

You can make a "one over one" response with a minimum responding hand (6 to 9 points). Do not respond 1 No trump, if you can respond "one over one."

3   4 Hearts. This hand contains 8 points as dummy in support of your partner's suit—7 points in high cards and 1 point for the doubleton.

Your partner's rebid indicates that he has a strong opening hand (16 to 18 points) and invites you to go on to game. With 8 or 9 points and more than adequate trump support, go to 4 Hearts.

4   2 Hearts. This hand contains 8 points as dummy in support of your partner's Heart suit—7 points in high cards and 1 point for the doubleton.

You have more than adequate trump support and a minimum responding hand (6 to 9 points). You have the requirements for a single raise.

5   2 Diamonds. This hand contains 8 points as dummy in support of your partner's Diamond suit—7 points in high cards and 1 point for the doubleton.

There is no game in the hand. Your partner's rebid indicates that he has a minimum opening hand (13 to 15 points). He does not invite you to rebid.

However, you prefer your partner's Diamond suit and must go back to Diamonds. Your rebid in Diamonds shows a mere preference, not a true raise.

6   Pass. This hand contains 8 points in support of your partner's Spade suit—7 points in high cards and 1 point for the doubleton.

A free raise requires more points than required to raise an opening bid. Even with adequate trump support, at least 9 or 10 points are required.

7   3 No trump. This hand contains 7 points in high cards. Your partner's jump rebid in a new suit indicates that he has a powerful opening hand (22 points and up). It forces you to keep the bidding open until game is reached.

You cannot raise either of your partner's suits. You cannot rebid your Hearts. Therefore bid 3 No trump.

1 1 Spade. This hand contains 11 points—8 points in high cards, 1 point for the doubleton, and 2 points for the singleton.

With a minimum responding hand (6 to 9 points) or more, you can respond "one over one."

2 1 Spade. This hand contains 11 points—8 points in high cards, 1 point for the doubleton and 2 points for the singleton.

With a minimum responding hand (6 to 9 points) or more, you can respond "one over one."

Do not respond 2 Diamonds. This hand is too strong for a single raise.

Do not respond 3 Diamonds. You must have a very strong responding hand (13 to 15 points) for a jump response of 3 Diamonds.

3 2 Spades. This hand contains 11 points—8 points in high cards, 1 point for the doubleton, and 2 points for the singleton.

With a strong responding hand (10 to 12 points), your hand is worth at least 1 rebid. Rebid your strong rebiddable Spade suit.

4 3 Spades. This hand contains 11 points—8 points in high cards, 1 point for the doubleton, and 2 points for the singleton.

This hand has all the requirements for a preemptive opening bid of 3 in a major.

You cannot open with a bid of 1 in a suit. You have approximately 10 points, but less than 10 points in high cards. You have a six-card suit.

5 Pass. This hand contains 11 points—8 points in high cards, 1 point for the doubleton, and 2 points for the singleton.

Preemptive opening bids are made with comparatively weak hands. Therefore, if your partner makes a preemptive opening bid, do not respond unless your own hand is strong enough for an opening bid of your own (13 to 15 points or more).

Even though your hand will not help your partner, do not bid your own suit in order to rescue him.

6 1 Spade. This hand contains 11 points—8 points in high cards, 1 point for the doubleton, and 2 points for the singleton.

With 10 to 12 points and a rebiddable suit, you can make a minimum overcall. When you contemplate making an overcall, the strength of your trump suit is the most important thing to consider.

7 Pass. This hand contains 11 points—8 points in high cards, 1 point for the doubleton, and 2 points for the singleton.

After your partner has made a take-out double, you should pass only when you have great length and strength in your opponent's suit and expect to set the contract. You must be able to take at least 4 tricks, and 3 of these tricks should be in the trump suit.

8 4 Spades. This hand contains 8 points in high cards. You have a 6-card Spade suit. When you have 8 or 9 points in high cards and a 6-card major suit, jump to 4 in your suit.

ANSWERS TO QUIZ 21

1 2 Diamonds. This hand contains 11 points—9 points in high cards and 1 point for each doubleton.

Your hand is too strong for a single raise in Spades.

With a strong responding hand (10 to 12 points), you can make a "two over one" response.

With a strong responding hand (10 to 12 points), you can rebid at least once. Even though you can support your partner's major suit, show your own suit first and raise your partner's suit when you rebid.

2 3 Spades. This hand contains 11 points—9 points in high cards and 1 point for each doubleton.

When your partner rebids his Spades, yon know that the hand should be played with Spades as trumps.

Your partner's rebid of 2 Spades indicates that he has a minimum opening hand (13 to 15 points).

You cannot be sure that you have 26 points in your combined hands. However, when you have a strong responding hand (10 to 12 points), your hand is worth 2 bids, so raise your partner to 3 Spades.

3 3 Diamonds. This hand contains 11 points—9 points in high cards and 1 point for each doubleton.

It meets all requirements for a preemptive opening bid of 3.

You cannot open with a bid of 1 in a suit. You have approximately 10 points, but less than 10 points in high cards. You have a six-card minor suit in which you hold 2 of the 3 top honors.

4 2 Diamonds. This hand contains 11 points—9 points in high cards and 1 point for each doubleton.

With 10 to 12 points or more and a long, strong suit, you have a safe overcall even at the level of 2. When you overcall at the level of 2, you tell your partner that you do not expect to lose more than 2 trump tricks. Your overcall invites your partner to lead Diamonds when he gets a chance.

5 2 Spades. This hand contains 11 points—9 points in high cards and 1 point for each doubleton.

More strength is required to respond to an overcall than to respond to an opening bid. At least a strong responding hand (10 to 12 points) should be held. Adequate trump support for an overcall is 1 trump less than required to support an opening bid.

If you have adequate trump support for your partner's suit, it is usually better to raise your partner than to bid a suit of your own. This is especially true if your partner's suit is a major suit and your own suit is a minor.

6 2 Diamonds. This hand contains 11 points—9 points in high cards and 1 point for each doubleton.

A free bid in a new suit at the level of 2 requires a strong responding hand (10 to 12 points).

ANSWERS TO QUIZ 22

1 1 No trump. This hand contains 11 points—10 points in high cards and 1 point for the doubleton.

With a strong responding hand (10 to 12 points), you can respond to a minimum overcall.

You cannot raise your partner's Spades. You cannot bid Diamonds, because your Diamond suit is not rebiddable. You have a stopper in your opponent's Club suit, so bid 1 No trump.

2 2 Diamonds. This hand contains 11 points—10 points in high cards and 1 point for the doubleton.

To make a "two over one" response, you must have a strong responding hand (10 to 12 points) and a biddable suit.

Your Diamond suit and Club suit are both biddable. Bid the higher ranking suit first.

3 3 No trump. This hand contains 10 points in high cards. It is a balanced hand.

If you hold a balanced hand with 10 to 14 points, raise your partner to 3 No trump.

You know your partner has at least 16 points, so you have at least 26 points in the combined hands. Therefore, you can make game.

4 3 No trump. This hand contains 10 points in high cards. Your partner's rebid at the level of 3 indicates that he holds a strong opening hand (16 to 18 points).

You have the 26 points necessary for a game. Even though you have no stopper in the Heart suit, take a chance on 3 No trump.

5 3 Clubs. This hand contains 11 points—10 points in high cards and 1 point for the doubleton.

With a strong responding hand (10 to 12 points) your hand is worth 2 bids.

You prefer Clubs to Spades. Do not rebid 2 Clubs, which would show a mere preference and would be a sign-off bid. A jump to 3 Clubs is necessary to show that you have a good raise.

6 Pass. This hand contains 10 points in high cards.

Preemptive bids are made with comparatively weak hands. You should not respond unless you have enough strength to make on opening bid of your own (13 to 15 points) or more.

7 3 Hearts. This hand contains 11 points—10 points in high cards and 1 point for the doubleton. Three small Hearts are adequate trump support for your partner's overcall.

With a strong responding hand (10 to 12 points) and adequate trump support, you can raise your partner's minimum overcall.

You cannot bid Diamonds, because your Diamond suit is not rebiddable.

ANSWERS TO QUIZ 23

1 3 No trump. This hand contains 10 points in high cards. Your partner's rebid invites you to go on. It indicates that he has a strong opening hand (16 to 18 points).

Since you have 10 points, game is in sight. You have a balanced hand, so bid 3 No trump.

If your partner has a long Spade suit, he will return to 4 Spades. Although your hand is really too strong for a single raise on your first response, you have no other response you can make.

2 1 No trump. This hand contains 10 points in high cards. It has a sure stopper in your opponent's suit.

If your partner makes a take-out double and then the opener's partner redoubles, you are no longer forced to bid. Even though you pass, your partner will have another chance to bid.

However, you have more than enough strength to bid. A free bid in this situation can be made with slightly less than a minimum responding hand (6 to 9 points). Your bid of 1 No trump shows your sure stopper in opponent's suit and indicates that you have no strong desire to name the trump suit.

ANSWERS TO QUIZ 23

3 2 Clubs. This hand contains 10 points in high cards. It has adequate trump support for your partner's Club suit.

A single raise can be given with a minimum responding hand (6 to 9 points) and adequate trump support. Although your hand is really too strong for a single raise, you have no other bid you can make on your first response.

4 1 No trump. This hand contains 10 points in high cards. You have a sure stopper in your opponent's suit.

When your partner makes a take-out double, you have a good No trump response if you hold a strong responding hand (10 to 12 points) and a stopper in your opponent's suit.

5 3 No trump. This hand contains 10 points in high cards. Your partner's rebid indicates that he has a strong opening hand (16 to 18 points) and invites you to go on. You can count 26 points in the combined hands, so game is in sight. Your hand is well suited to No trump play, so bid 3 No trump.

With a strong responding hand (10 to 12 points), your hand is worth at least 2 bids.

Although your hand is really too strong for a single raise on your first response, you have no other response you can make.

6 1 No trump. This hand contains 10 points in high cards. A free bid of 1 No trump requires a strong responding hand (10 to 12 points) and a stopper in opponent's suit.

ANSWERS TO QUIZ 24

1 Pass. This hand contains 3 points in high cards.
Even though you have more than adequate trump support, you cannot give your partner a single raise, unless you have a minimum responding hand (6 to 9 points).

2 2 No trump. This hand contains 3 points in high cards.
The opening bid of 2 in a suit is forcing to game. You must bid no matter how weak your hand may be.
If you have less than 8 points, respond by bidding 2 No trump, no matter what your distribution may be. A response of 2 No trump is a negative response.
For a positive response 8 points are required.

3 Pass. This hand contains 3 points in high cards.
Because your right hand opponent inserted a bid, you are no longer forced to respond to your partner's take-out double. In this case, a free bid, even at the level of 1, requires at least a minimum responding hand (6 to 9 points).

4 Pass. This hand contains 3 points in high cards.
When your partner has bid 2 suits, prefer the suit in which you have the greater length. In this case show your preference by passing. There is no need to raise the Diamonds to show your preference.

5 Pass. This hand contains 3 points in high cards. It is a balanced hand. The opening bid of 2 No trump is not forcing. You must have 4 points with a balanced hand to raise to 3 No trump.

6 1 Diamond. This hand contains 3 points in high cards.
When your partner makes a take-out double, you must respond, no matter how weak your hand may be. You can pass only when you have great length and strength in your opponent's suit and expect to set the contract.

7 Pass. This hand contains 3 points in high cards.

If your partner makes a take-out double and your right hand opponent redoubles, you are no longer forced to bid. If you have less than a minimum responding hand (6 to 9 points) do not make a free bid, unless you have a strong desire to name the trump suit.

ANSWERS TO QUIZ 25

1 1 No trump. This hand contains 7 points—6 points in high cards and 1 point for the doubleton.

You cannot respond "two over one" because you do not have a strong responding hand (10 to 12 points).

You cannot give a single raise, because you do not have adequate trump support.

However, with a minimum responding hand (6 to 9 points) in high cards and a balanced hand, you can keep the bidding open by responding 1 No trump.

2 3 No trump. This hand contains 6 points in high cards. Your partner's jump rebid in a new suit forces you to keep the bidding open until game is reached.

You do not have adequate trump support for either of your partner's 2 suits. With strength in the 2 unbid suits and No trump distribution, bid 3 No trump.

3 3 Diamonds. This hand contains 7 points—6 points in high cards and 1 point for the doubleton. As dummy for a No trump contract, your hand is worth only 6 points, because no points are counted for short suits. Your 3 Diamond bid shows that you prefer Diamonds to No trump. It shows a mere preference, not a true raise. It does not encourage your partner to try for game.

ANSWERS TO QUIZ 25

4 3 No trump. This hand contains 6 points in high cards. It is a balanced hand.

With 4 points and a balanced hand, respond 3 No trump.

5 Pass. This hand contains 7 points—6 in high cards and 1 for the doubleton. Do not respond to a jump overcall unless you have a very strong responding hand (13 to 15 points).

However, if you know that your partner (not up-to-date) still uses a jump overcall as a strong bid and not a preemptive bid, respond 2 No trump.

6 Pass. This hand contains 7 points—6 points in high cards and 1 point for the doubleton.

This hand is not strong enough for a free bid. At least 9 or 10 points are required for a free raise. You do not have to bid to keep the bidding open. Your partner will have another chance to bid.

7 2 Spades. This hand contains 7 points—6 points in high cards and 1 point for the doubleton.

With 6 or 7 points, the responding hand should not rebid unless forced to do so.

Nevertheless, when your partner has opened the bidding in one suit and has rebid in a second suit, you must show which of his suits you prefer. Therefore, in this case you are forced to bid again in order to return to the suit your partner bid first. Your bid shows a mere preference, not a true raise.

ANSWERS TO QUIZ 26

1 2 Spades. This hand contains 19 points—16 points in high cards, 1 point for the doubleton, and 2 points for the singleton.

When your partner has opened by bidding 1 in a suit and you have a tremendous responding hand (19 to 21 points), make a jump response in a new suit.

A jump response in a new suit is an invitation to slam.

2 1 Spade. This hand contains 19 points—16 points in high cards, 1 point for the doubleton, and 2 points for the singleton.

With 14 points you must open. With 2 suits of equal length, bid the higher ranking suit first.

Do not open 2 Spades. You do not have enough points for an opening bid of 2 in a suit.

3 3 Diamonds. This hand contains 19 points—16 points in high cards, 1 point for the doubleton, and 2 points for the singleton.

Your partner's response of 1 No trump is discouraging. Nevertheless, if you have a very strong opening hand (19 to 21 points), you should give a jump rebid after your partner's response of 1 No trump.

A jump rebid in a new suit forces your partner to keep the bidding open until game is reached.

4 3 Diamonds. This hand contains 19 points—16 points in high cards, 1 point for the doubleton, and 2 points for the singleton.

A rebid of 3 in a new suit requires at least a strong opening hand (16 to 19 points).

When 2 five-card suits are held, bid the higher ranking suit first and show the lower ranking suit on the first rebid. Then rebid the lower ranking suit before rebidding your higher suit.

5 Double. This hand contains 19 points—16 ponits in high cards, 1 point for the doubleton, and 2 points for the singleton.

Make a take-out double. If your partner responds 2 Clubs bid your Spades on the second round.

ANSWERS TO QUIZ 27

1 1 Spade. This hand contains 19 points—17 points in high cards and 2 points for the singleton.

With 14 points you must open.

Do not open with a bid of 2 Spades. An opening bid of 2 in a suit requires 23 points with a strong six-card suit.

2 2 Spades. This hand contains 19 points—17 points in high cards and 2 points for the singleton.

With a tremendous responding hand (19 to 21 points) and a long, strong suit, make a jump response in a new suit. This jump response in a new suit is forcing to game and invites a slam.

3 4 Spades. This hand contains 19 points—17 points in high cards and 2 points for the singleton.

Do not rebid 2 Spades. If you do, your partner will pass. With a very strong opening hand (19 to 21 points) and a strong six-card major suit, jump to 4 in your major suit.

4 4 Spades. This hand contains 19 points—17 points in high cards and 2 points for the singleton.

With a very strong opening hand (19 to 21 points) and a strong six-card major suit, jump to 4 in your suit.

5 4 Spades. This hand contains 19 points—17 points in high cards and 2 points for the singleton.

Do not rebid 2 Spades or even 3 Spades. With a very strong opening hand (19 to 21 points) and a strong, six-card major suit, jump to 4 in your own major suit.

Your partner's "two over one" response indicates that he has at least 10 points. You know that there are at least 29 points in the combined hands. Your rebid of 4 Spades does not sign off. Your partner may want to explore the possibility of a slam.

6 Double. This hand contains 19 points—17 points in high cards and 2 points for the singleton.

Make a take-out double. You have good trump support for any suit your partner may bid.

Show your Spades on the second round of bidding.

7 6 Spades. This hand contains 17 points in high cards.

It contains a long, strong Spade suit. With 17 or 18 points in high cards, jump to slam in a long, strong suit.

ANSWERS TO QUIZ 28

1 1 Club. This hand contains 21 points—19 points in high cards and 1 point for each doubleton.

With 14 points you must open. With 2 suits of unequal length, bid the longer suit first.

Do not open with 2 Clubs. For an opening bid of 2 in a suit, 25 points are required with a strong five-card suit.

ANSWERS TO QUIZ 28

2 4 Spades. This hand contains 21 points—19 points in high cards and 1 point for each doubleton.

With a very strong opening hand (19 to 21 points) and four-card support for your partner's major suit, jump to 4 in partner's suit.

This is not a shut-out bid. A raise from 1 to 4 by the opening bidder is stronger than a raise of 1 to 3.

3 3 Clubs. This hand contains 21 points—19 points in high cards and 1 point for each doubleton.

When your partner has made an opening bid of 1 in a suit and you have a tremendous responding hand (19 to 21 points), make a jump response in a new suit. This jump response in a new suit invites a slam.

4 3 Spades. This hand contains 21 points—19 points in high cards and 1 point for each doubleton.

After a response of 1 No trump by your partner, if you have a very strong opening hand (19 to 21 points), you should either jump to game or force your partner to keep the bidding open until game is reached by making a jump rebid in a new suit.

5 3 Spades. This hand contains 21 points—19 points in high cards and 1 point for each doubleton.

When your partner gives you a single raise, if you have a very strong opening hand (19 to 21 points), you should either jump to game in your suit or force your partner to keep the bidding open until game is reached by making a jump rebid in a new suit.

6 2 No trump. This hand contains 19 points in high cards. When your partner responds "one over one," you can jump to 2 No trump, if you have a very strong opening hand (19 to 21 points) and a hand suited to No trump play.

ANSWERS TO QUIZ 29

1 1 Spade. This hand contains 8 points—7 points in high cards and 1 point for the doubleton.

With a minimum responding hand (6 to 9 points), ignore the double and bid as though the take-out doubler had passed.

If your opponent had not doubled, you would have responded 1 Spade, because you have a minimum responding hand (6 to 9 points) and a biddable suit.

2 2 No trump. This hand contains 8 points—7 points in high cards and 1 additional point because the hand contains a five-card suit. It is a balanced hand.

With 8 or 9 points, raise to 2 No trump.

However, if you know that your partner is an advanced player and that he uses the 2 Club Convention, respond 2 Clubs to show that your hand contains 8 or more points and a 4 card or longer major suit.

3 Pass. This hand contains 8 points—7 points in high cards and 1 point for the doubleton.

Your partner's rebid shows a minimum opening hand (13 to 15 points) and does not invite you to go on. With 8 or 9 points, rebid only if invited to do so. Therefore, pass.

4 1 Spade. This hand contains 8 points—7 points in high cards and 1 point for the doubleton.

When your right hand opponent inserts a bid after a take-out double by your partner, you are no longer forced to bid.

However, if you hold a minimum responding hand (6 to 9 points), you have adequate strength for a free response at the level of. 1

ANSWERS TO QUIZ 29

5 Pass. This hand contains 8 points—7 points in high cards and 1 point for the doubleton.

There is no reason to bid unless you have a chance for game. Therefore, you should have at least a strong responding hand (10 to 12 points) to make a positive response to a minimum overcall.

6 Pass. This hand contains 8 points—7 points in high cards and 1 point for the doubleton in Hearts (which can be counted if you are considering a bid in Spades). Do not respond to a jump overcall, unless you have a very strong responding hand (13 to 15 points).

However, if you know that your partner (not up-to-date) still uses a jump overcall as a strong bid and not a preemptive bid, respond much the same as you would to an opening bid of 1 in a suit. With 6 to 9 points you can respond in a higher ranking suit at the same level. Bid 2 Spades.

7 2 Spades. This hand contains 8 points—7 points in high cards and 1 point for the doubleton.

When your right hand opponent inserts a bid after a take-out double by your partner, you are no longer forced to bid. However, with a minimum responding hand (6 to 9 points) and a good major suit, you have ample strength for a free bid even at the level of 2.

ANSWERS TO QUIZ 30

1 1 Spade. This hand contains 9 points—7 points in high cards and 2 points for the singleton.

Even at the level of 1, a free response requires more points than the minimum required to make a "one over one" response to an opening bid.

A free response at the level of 1 should not be made with less than 9 points.

2 2 No trump. This hand contains 8 points—7 points in high cards and 1 additional point for the five-card suit. Do not count any points for the singleton when your partner opens 1 No trump. With 8 or 9 points, bid 2 No trump.

However, if you know that your partner is an advanced player and that he uses the 2 Club Convention, respond 2 Clubs to show that your hand contains 8 or more points and a 4 card or longer major suit.

3 2 Spades. This hand contains 9 points—7 points in high cards and 2 points for the singleton.
With 8 points, you can make a positive response.

4 1 Spade. This hand contains 9 points—7 points in high cards and 2 points for the singleton.
If your partner makes a take-out double and the opener's partner redoubles, you are no longer forced to bid. However, if you have a five-card suit, you want to show it. With such a suit, you can make a free bid with less than 6 to 9 points, because you have a strong desire to name the trump suit.

5 Pass. This hand contains 9 points—7 points in high cards and 2 points for the singleton.
You should have at least 10 to 12 points and a strong trump suit to justify an overcall. Your Spade suit is much too weak for an overcall. You should have a rebiddable suit for an overcall even at the level of 1.

6 2 No trump. This hand contains 8 points—7 points in high cards and 1 additional point for the five-card suit. The requirements for a response to an overcall of 1 No trump are the same as the requirements for a response to an opening bid of 1 No trump.

However, if you know that your partner is an advanced player and that he uses the 2 Club Convention, respond 2 Clubs to show that your hand contains 8 or more points and a 4 card or longer major suit.

ANSWERS TO QUIZ 30

7 1 Spade. This hand contains 9 points—7 points in high cards and 2 points for the singleton.

When your partner has doubled the opening bid, and opener's partner inserts a bid, you are no longer forced to respond.

If you have a minimum responding hand (6 to 9 points), however, you are justified in making a free response to your partner's take-out double.

ANSWERS TO QUIZ 31

1 3 Spades. This hand contains 10 points—9 points in high cards and 1 point for the doubleton.

With a strong responding hand (10 to 12 points), you should rebid at least once.

Even though your partner's rebid indicates that he has a minimum opening hand (13 to 15 points), keep the bidding open.

2 2 Spades. This hand contains 10 points—9 points in high cards and 1 point for the doubleton.

With a strong responding hand (10 to 12 points), you are strong enough to respond to a minimum overcall, if you do so without raising the level of the bidding.

You cannot raise your partner's Club suit with only 2 small trumps. You have a good rebiddable major suit of your own which you can bid without raising the level of the bidding.

3 3 Spades. This hand contains 10 points—9 points in high cards and 1 additional point for the five-card suit.

With 10 to 14 points and a long, strong suit, jump to 3 in your suit. This jump response is forcing to game.

4 1 Spade. This hand contains 10 points—9 points in high cards and 1 point for the doubleton.

A Spade lead from your partner is desired.

You have the requirements for a minimum overcall—a strong responding hand (10 to 12 points) with a rebiddable suit.

Your overcall of 1 Spade tells your partner to lead Spades if he gets a chance.

5 1 Spade. This hand contains 10 points—9 points in high cards and 1 point for the doubleton.

With a strong responding hand (10 to 12 points), you have more than enough to make a free response at the level of 1.

6 2 Spades. This hand contains 10 points—9 points in high cards and 1 point for the doubleton.

With a strong responding hand (10 to 12 points), you should rebid at least once. Your Spade suit is rebiddable. But your hand is not strong enough for a jump to 3 Spades.

7 2 Hearts. This hand contains 10 points—9 points in high cards and 1 point for the doubleton. With 3 small trumps, you have adequate support for your partner's overcall in Hearts. Normal trump support for an overcall is 1 trump less than that required to support an opening bid.

With a strong responding hand (10 to 12 points), and adequate trump support, you can raise your partner's minimum overcall.

Do not change the suit if you can support your partner's suit, unless your partner has bid a minor suit and you have a strong rebiddable major.

ANSWERS TO QUIZ 32

1 2 Hearts. This hand contains 13 points—12 points in high cards and 1 point for the doubleton.

With 10 to 12 points or more and a strong Heart suit, you can safely overcall 2 Hearts.

Do not make a take-out-double. Your only chance of outbidding your opponents is in the Heart suit.

2 Pass. This hand contains 13 points—12 points in high cards and 1 point for the doubleton.

When you open the bidding with a minimum opening hand (13 to 15 points), and your partner responds 1 No trump, rebid only for safety. You have a balanced hand suitable for a No trump contract. Don't rebid even though you have a strong rebiddable Heart suit.

3 Pass. This hand contains 13 points—12 points in high cards and 1 point for the doubleton. It has a strong rebiddable Heart suit.

Preemptive opening bids are made with comparatively weak hands. Therefore, if your partner makes a preemptive opening bid do not respond in a suit of your own, unless you have 16 to 18 points and a very strong rebiddable major suit.

4 Double. This hand contains 13 points—12 points in high cards and 1 point for the doubleton.

At least 13 to 15 points are required for a take-out double.

If your partner should respond 1 Spade, you can support his Spade suit.

If your partner should respond in Clubs, you have a strong rebiddable Heart suit in which you can safely play the hand.

ANSWERS TO QUIZ 32

5   4 No trump. This hand contains 13 points—12 points in high cards and 1 point for the doubleton.

Your partner's jump rebid indicates that he has a very strong opening hand (19 to 21 points). Therefore, you probably have 33 points in the combined hands. Your partner has a strong Spade suit which you can support. You have a strong side suit in Hearts. Therefore, explore the possibility of a slam.

When you hold a responding hand which is as good as an opening bid, if your partner opens the bidding and later jumps, be alert for a slam.

ANSWERS TO QUIZ 33

1   3 No trump. This hand contains 8 points in high cards. It does not contain a biddable suit.

With 8 points but no biddable suit, respond 3 No trump. This jump to 3 No trump is a positive response. It is not a negative response like 2 No trump.

2   Pass. This hand contains 8 points in high cards. Do not respond to a jump overcall unless you have a very strong responding hand (13 to 15 points).

However, if you know that your partner (not up-to-date) still uses a jump overcall as a strong bid and not a preemptive bid, respond much the same as you would to an opening bid of 1 in a suit. With 6 to 9 points in high cards and a stopper in your opponent's suit you can make a No trump bid at the same level. Respond 3 No trump. Do not raise your partner to 4 Clubs. You can probably stop your opponent's Diamond suit twice. It should be easier to make 3 No trump than 5 Clubs.

ANSWERS TO QUIZ 33

3 1 No trump. This hand contains 8 points in high cards. When your partner's opening bid has been doubled by your right hand opponent, you ignore the double, if you have a minimum responding hand (6 to 9 points).
If your opponent had not made a take-out double, you would have responded 1 No trump.

4 3 No trump. This hand contains 8 points in high cards. Your partner's rebid invites you to go on. It indicates that he has a very strong opening hand (19 to 21 points). You have at least 27 points, enough for game, in the combined hands. Your hand is well suited to No trump play, so bid 3 No trump. With 8 or 9 points, rebid if invited.

5 2 Spades. This hand contains 8 points in high cards. When your partner has opened 1 in a suit and on his rebid has named a second suit, you must show in which of these 2 suits you think the two hands combined hold the most trumps. When you hold the same number of cards in each of your partner's suits, you should prefer the suit he bid first, even though you have better cards in your partner's second suit. Your rebid in this case shows a mere preference, not a true raise.

6 3 Hearts. This hand contains 8 points. It has adequate support for your partner's Heart suit.
You have 8 points—the minimum required for a positive response.
When your partner has opened with 2 in a suit and you have 8 points or more and adequate support for his suit, the best possible response is a raise in his suit.

7 Pass. This hand contains 8 points in high cards. It has adequate trump support for your partner's Heart suit. However, at least 9 or 10 points are required for a free raise.

ANSWERS TO QUIZ 34

1 2 No trump. This hand contains 22 points in high cards. It meets all the requirements for an opening bid of 2 No trump—22 to 24 points in high cards, a balanced hand, and a sure stopper in every suit.

Do not open 2 in a suit. You do not have a strong enough trump suit.

2 4 No trump. This hand contains 23 points—22 points in high cards and 1 point for the doubleton.

When your partner opens with a preemptive bid of 3 in a suit, explore the possibility of a slam, if you hold a powerful responding hand (16 to 18 points) or more, including 3 Aces, or 2 Aces and the K or Q of your partner's suit.

3 2 Hearts. This hand contains 23 points—22 points in high cards and 1 point for the doubleton.

With a tremendous responding hand (19 to 21 points), you should make a jump response in a new suit, if you have a long, strong suit or 4 of your partner's suit. With a hand as strong as this one, the jump shift should be given even though you do not have a long, strong suit of your own or 4 of your partner's suit.

A jump response in a new suit forces your partner to keep the bidding open until game is reached. It is an invitation to try for a slam.

ANSWER TO QUIZ 35

2 Hearts. This hand contains 25 points—24 points in high cards and 1 point for the doubleton.

It meets the requirements for an opening bid of 2 in a suit—25 points and a strong five-card suit.

Do not open 2 No trump. Even though the hand also meets the requirements for an opening bid of 2 No trump—22 to 24 points in high cards, balanced distribution, and a sure stopper in every suit—a bid of 2 in a suit is better.

ANSWER TO QUIZ 36

2 Spades. This hand contains 23 points—20 points in high cards, 1 point for the doubleton, and 2 points for the singleton.

With 23 points and a strong six-card suit, open with 2 in your suit.

Summary

POINTS FOR HIGH CARDS
A - 4   K - 3   Q - 2   J - 1

POINTS FOR DISTRIBUTION

When Bidding Your Own Suit	*When Raising Partner's Suit*
1 point - Doubleton - 1 point	
2 points - Singleton - 3 points	
3 points - Void - - - 5 points	

When Responding to Bid of 1 No trump
Add 1 point for a 5-card or longer suit

POINTS REQUIRED

26 - game in No trump	33 - small slam
26 - game in major suit	37 - grand slam
29 - game in minor suit	

Type of Hand

Opening Bidder	POINTS	Responding Bidder
	6 - 9	Minimum
	10 - 12	Strong
Minimum	13 - 15	Very Strong
Strong	16 - 18	Powerful
Very Strong	19 - 21	Tremendous
Powerful	22 & up	

DISTRIBUTION

Balanced Hand— (5-3-3-2) or (4-4-3-2) or (4-3-3-3)
Unbalanced Hand— Any other distribution

Type of Suit

Biddable

Any 4-card suit headed A, K, Q 10, or better
Any 5-card suit

Rebiddable

Any 5-card suit headed A J, KJ9, QJ9, or better
Any 6-card suit

Opening Bid of 1 In A Suit

13 points—Open with 1 rebiddable suit or 2 biddable suits
14 points—Open without fail

With suits of unequal length—Bid the longest suit first
With suits of   equal length—Bid the highest ranking suit first

---

Opening Bid of 2 In A Suit

25 points—With a strong 5-card suit
23 points—With a strong 6-card suit
21 points—With a strong 7-card suit

Opening Bid of 3 In A Suit

Without the requirements for an opening bid of 1 in a suit
With less than 10 points in high cards

10 points approximately
6 trumps if not vulnerable; 7 trumps if vulnerable
2 of the 3 top honors, if a minor suit is bid

Opening Bid of 1 No Trump

16 to 18 points in high cards only—No more & no less
Balanced hand—(5-3-3-2) or (4-4-3-2) or (4-3-3-3)
Doubleton—Kx or better
3 suits stopped

Opening Bid of 2 No Trump

22 to 24 points in high cards only—No more & no less
Balanced hand—(5-3-3-2) or (4-4-3-2) or (4-3-3-3)
All suits stopped

Response to Opening Bid of 1 in A Suit

Take-out of 1 No trump

6 to 9 points—in high cards only—No more & no less

Single Raise in Partner's Suit

6 to 9 points—With x x x x, Q x x, or J 10 x in trump suit

One over One - Suit Take-out

6 to 9 points—With a biddable suit

Two over One - Suit Take-out

10 to 12 points—With a biddable suit

Jump to 2 No Trump - Forcing

13 to 15 points—With balanced hand & stopper in all unbid suits

Jump to 3 in Partner's Suit - Forcing

13 to 15 points—With x x x x in trump suit

Jump in a New Suit - Forcing

19 to 21 points—With long strong suit, or
                With 4 of partner's suit

Response to Opening of 2 In A Suit

Less than 8 points	Bid 2 No trump
8 points—With no biddable suit	Bid 3 No trump
8 points—With a biddable suit	Bid your suit
8 points—With trump support	Bid 3 in partner's suit

Response to Opening of 3 In A Suit

When Partner Opens with 3 in Minor

16 to 18 points—With a strong rebiddable major..Bid 3 in major
13 to 15 points—With Ax, Kx, or Qx, in partner's suit.
        Bid 3 No trump

When Partner Opens With 3 in Major
13 to 15 points—Raise to 4—Even without trump support

Response to Opening Bid of 1 No Trump

0 to 5 points	Pass, or Bid 2 in long safe suit
6 to 9 points.. With 6 to 7 points	Pass, or Bid 2 in 5-card suit, or Bid 4 in 6-card major
With 8 to 9 points..	Bid 2 No trump, or Bid 4 in 6-card major
10 to 12 points	Bid 3 No trump, or
13 to 15 points	Bid 3 in long strong suit
16 to 18 points.. With only 16 points..	Bid 4 No trump
With 17 or 18 points..	Bid 6 No trump, or Bid 6 in long strong suit

---

Response to Opening Bid of 2 No Trump

Less than 4 points	Pass, or Bid 6-card major
4 points or more	Bid 3 No trump, or Bid 3 in 5-card major
10 points	Bid 4 No trump
11 or 12 points	Bid 6 No trump, or Bid 6 in long strong suit

Rebid by Opening Bidder
AFTER ORIGINAL OPENING BID OF 1 NO TRUMP

When Partner Responds 2 in a Suit

Less than 18 points		Pass
18 points . .	A maximum No trump & Strong trump support	Raise Partner

When Partner Responds 2 No Trump

16 points . .	A minimum No trump	Pass
More than 16 points		Rebid

When Partner Responds 4 No Trump

16 points . .	A minimum No trump	Pass
More than 16 points		Bid 6 No trump

Rebid by Opening Bidder
AFTER ORIGINAL BID OF 1 IN A SUIT

When Partner Responds with 1 No trump

13 to 15 points
16 to 18 points . . Pass or make a weak rebid for safety
19 to 21 points . . Jump

When Partner Responds with a Single Raise

13 to 15 points— Pass
16 to 18 points— Rebid
19 to 21 points— Jump

When Partner Responds (One Over One) or (Two Over One)

13 to 15 points
        Bid 1 in a new higher ranking suit
        Bid 1 No trump
        Bid 2 in any suit, except a new higher ranking suit
16 to 18 points
        Bid 2 in a new higher ranking suit
        Bid 2 No trump but don't jump
        Bid 3 in your own or in partner's suit
        Bid 3 in a new suit, but don't jump
19 to 21 points
        Jump in No trump
        Jump to 4 in your own or in partner's major suit
        Bid 2 in a new higher ranking suit
        Bid 3 in a new suit but don't jump
22 & up points
        Jump to 3 No trump after "1 over 1"
        Jump in a new suit

Rebid By Responder

After Original Bid of 1 in a Suit by Partner

6 to 9 points.. Rebid if forced—with 6 or 7 points
Rebid if invited—with 8 or 9 points

10 to 12 points.. Rebid at least once

13 to 15 points.. Jump in a suit already bid, or
Rebid in new suits until game is reached

16 to 18 points.. Make big jump rebid

19 to 21 points.. Explore slam

After Partner Has Bid 2 Suits - Show Preference

With unequal length—prefer your own longer suit
With equal length—prefer your partner's first suit

Minimum Overcall

10 to 12 points—With a rebiddable suit

Response to Minimum Overcall

No Trump Take-out

10 to 12 points.. With sure stopper in opponent's suit

Single Raise in Partner's Suit

10 to 12 points.. With 1 trump less than adequate support

Suit Take-out

10 to 12 points.. With a strong rebiddable suit—at same level
13 to 15 points.. With a strong rebiddable suit—at higher level

Strong Overcall

Take-out Double

13 to 15 points..	With support for all 3 suits not bid by opponent
16 to 18 points..	With a strong rebiddable suit

Jump Overcall

Approx. 10 points.	With 6 trumps if not vulnerable
	With 7 trumps if vulnerable

No Trump Overcall

16 to 18 points..	With requirements for opening bid of 1 No trump
	With sure stopper in opponent's suit

Response to Strong Overcall

When Partner Overcalls With 1 No Trump
Same as response to opening bid of 1 No trump

When Partner Makes Jump Overcall
13 to 15 points—Even without trump support—Raise partner

When Partner Makes Take-out Double

Great length and strength in opponent's suit......		Pass
0 to 9 points	....	Bid longest suit
10 to 12 points..	With stopper in opponent's suit.	Bid No trump
10 to 12 points..	With a biddable suit	Jump in a suit

---

Free Bids

When Partner Opens and Opponent Overcalls
10 to 12 points....... Make free response

When Partner Opens and Opponent Makes Take-out Double

10 to 12 points.......	Redouble
Otherwise	Ignore take-out double

*When Partner Makes Take-out Double and
Opponent Bids or Redoubles*

6 to 9 points.......	Respond if opponent bids
Even less	Respond if opponents redouble

Slam Bidding

Small Slam

33 points
A very strong trump suit
A strong side suit
1st-round control in 3 suits
2nd-round control in 4th suit

Grand Slam

37 points
A very strong trump suit
A strong side suit
1st-round control in all 4 suits

Double For Penalty

When you can set opponents 2 tricks, or
When your partner opens and your opponent's overcall is the same
as the response you expected to make